THE ACTIVE *seniors* GUIDE TO *budget* WORLD TRAVEL

RACHEL S. IMPER

THE ACTIVE SENIORS GUIDE TO BUDGET WORLD TRAVEL

Cover illustration by Lillian Jackson

Disclaimer: The material in this book cannot substitute for professional advice; further, while great care was taken to make the material in this book as accurate possible, travel information changes frequently. The author cannot be held liable if the reader relied on the material and was financially damaged in any way.

Print ISBN: 978-1-54390-274-7

eBook ISBN: 97-8-154390-275-4

Printed in the United States of America by BookBaby Books

For Kevin, my favorite travel companion, and all the journeys we have taken together.

TABLE OF CONTENTS

ACKNOWLEDGMENTS

The following people and organizations have earned my immense gratitude for their significant contributions to this book.

For their excellent suggestions, reviews, and support:

Marie Bogan	Kevin G. Imper
Margery Ellsworth	Eric Mathison
Kathryn Gillett	Wes Neuenschwander
Jeanie Harris	Barb Renard
Keara Holm-Nielsen	Kathy Webb
Carol Imper	

For her wonderful illustration and cover design:

Lillian Jackson

For information on health resources abroad:

Brian Donohue, UW Medicine Strategic Marketing and Communications

Justin Harford, Mobility International USA

Cheryl Lake, Northwest Kidney Centers

INTRODUCTION

When I set out to plan our nearly three-month trip to Paris (and our round-the-world trip a year later), I found that most budget travel guides were either written for a much younger audience, or they were intended for a vacation of only a few weeks or less. But now that my husband and I are retired, we want to travel for a longer time. While many sources were helpful, they didn't give me enough information all in one place.

That's why I wrote this book. If you're like most active seniors, you still have a sense of adventure but you don't have much in common with a young vagabond. You don't want to wrestle with a large backpack and risk hurting your back. And having your bathroom down the hall isn't practical when bladder or prostate issues, so common in our age group, means you often have to get up in the night. You want a little more comfort, quiet, and privacy than you did at twenty, but you still need to tightly manage your budget.

Seniors have other concerns too, especially when taking a longer trip. Issues such as renewing prescriptions, knowing what to do if you get sick, finding travel health insurance if you're over 70, and discovering the age limits of your car-rental company are all important to work out in advance. Having the answers can help you travel more confidently.

This book is intended to help seniors who are planning either a long-term trip in one or more locations or a round-the-world trip, although I hope it will be helpful for short-term travel too. I don't consider myself a travel guru, but I hope my research will give you a head start planning your own adventures.

How to use this book:

This book is not meant to be the *only* one you will need to plan your dream trip. It's intended to work with popular guidebooks and other information. With this book, you can:

- Gain the inspiration and knowledge to travel the world affordably on your own.

- Discover a range of resources to help you confidently plan your trip, along with tips and tricks unique to this book.

- Get access to a website with updates and give you a way to offer feedback to help others.

Who is an "active senior"?

My definition of an active senior is anyone over the age of 55 who is mostly mobile. (If you have more serious challenges, you will find additional references in the Appendix.) You are an active senior if you can walk at least a half hour at a moderate pace — with or without a cane — but maybe you can't easily climb more than one flight of stairs. You may be strong and free of illness, or you may have a few chronic health problems. You may have to take daily medications, require regular blood testing (for example, if you are taking warfarin), or need blood-pressure monitoring, but you are mostly able and eager to travel.

If you meet these requirements and can answer yes to any of the questions below, then this book is for you:

- You like foreign travel, but now that you're retired, your travel budget has shrunk, and you could use some tips on traveling inexpensively.

- You would like to travel independently, but aren't quite sure how to do it — or you feel a little overwhelmed at the idea.

- You want to extend a tour with independent travel on your own.

- You want to live for a month or more in a foreign country or countries.

- You're planning a once-in-a-lifetime, round-the-world trip.

- If there's one thing I hope this book can do, it is to let you know you can make your travel dreams come true — and for less money than you may think. If you can travel without major problems in the United States and Canada, you can travel successfully most places in the world — and you won't have to live in a tent! (Unless you want to.)

One caveat: To get the most out of this book, you need to be familiar with the Internet. I also recommend taking a tablet computer with you on your journey. A smartphone may work, but, if you're like me, you'll find that, with aging eyes, web pages are much easier to read on a tablet or laptop. If you're not technically savvy or are afraid of using online services, see the section in the Appendix, "Master the Online World."

If you need additional help...

I have also noted some resources in the Appendix for people of color, LGBTQ travelers, and solo women adventurers. While I wish we lived in a world where diversity and tolerance were cherished everywhere, and people weren't at risk of discrimination, I know the world is not always as we would like it to be. I hope these resources will help you find the kind of connections that make your journey as rewarding as possible.

Yes, you can make your dreams come true!

My husband, Kevin, and I have traveled extensively both before and after our retirement, in Europe, Asia, Africa, Australia, and New Zealand. (We have taken several trips to Mexico, but we have only touched up against South America, which is still on the agenda.) During our careers, we have lived for months at a time in Europe and in Asia. To see more, we often move from location to location on our trips, but we mostly like to settle in one place for weeks at a time — which is one of the best ways to save money.

I assume that if you are a senior planning independent travel to the more remote areas of the world, you are probably an experienced traveler who won't need many tips, so this book may be less useful to you. And though I feel confident the strategies in this book can serve you well just about anywhere in the world, it is primarily focused on travel to common tourist destinations.

Kevin and I don't have a trust fund or a sizeable retirement package. Our IRAs would inspire little envy. Our savings are small, and our Social Security is close to average, so we need all the help we can get to travel.

If we can do it, so can you.
Let me show you how...

Note: My apologies to my friends outside of the United States, especially my Canadian neighbors. This book has a natural bias in favor of US travelers, simply because I am a US citizen and much of this research was done planning my own trips. I do hope you will still find it useful. I would also like to hear from readers and will incorporate suggestions in any subsequent editions. Submit your suggestions at www. seniorbudgettravel.com.

All prices in this book, except where noted, are quoted in US dollars, as of late 2016 or early 2017.

CHAPTER 1:

PLANNING YOUR DREAM TRIP

Here's a view of Gardens by the Bay, Singapore. The world awaits!

What kind of trip do you want? While this book is aimed primarily at seniors who want to travel for a month or more, you can also use it to plan shorter trips abroad or to supplement a tour. But where do you want to go and what type of travel do you really want?

Get inspired with these six tips!

Have some places in mind where you'd like to go? Here are some tips to get started. Then, check the recommendations at the end of this chapter.

- Read travel books and magazines. You can get them at the library to save money. (Later, you may want to buy a few if your library doesn't have the most recent editions, but you probably won't need the latest ones at this point.) Look not only at the guides, but also at the coffee-table books, which feature large photos of travel locales.

- Search the Internet. Most countries and large cities have official websites with valuable information for travelers. (Search "[name of city/country] + official website.")

- Follow travel blogs and expat forums to get a sense of what others like or dislike. (Some of my best travel tips for specific destinations have come from travel blogs.)

- Do web searches on tours in the regions you are interested in. (The idea is not that you will necessarily take the tours, but by reading where the tours go, you can identify the must-sees at your chosen destinations. After that, you can branch out.)

- Talk to friends and others who have traveled to destinations that appeal to you. If you like a lot of the same things, then they may well be your best travel advisors.

- Think about your interests. It's one thing to book a tour designed to fit many travelers, but it's another entirely if you have a hobby or engage in a sport or special interest. If you like to kayak or cycle, search for tours that focus on those activities. If you like to garden, seek out garden tours. A weaver? Look for local guilds. (You get the idea. Traveling independently will give you the opportunity to have an itinerary that's customized for you.)

Banish the Nervous Nellies!

Whatever you do, when you're planning a trip, especially a round-the-world excursion or long-term journey, don't listen to the naysayers. Remember that the world really is full of kind people, and everywhere we have gone — without exception — we have never failed to encounter people who were eager to help when we asked. As long as you have your passport, a credit card, and your critical medications, most problems can be resolved. (And even if those things get lost, there is almost always someone who can help.)

Travel mistakes can add spice to your journey.

When traveling on our own, we find there are bound to be a few minor glitches along the way. Those travel mistakes have sometimes provided us with cherished experiences, or at least something to chuckle over later on.

We missed the boat! (Or at least, our stop.)

Once, in Malaysia, we missed our ferry stop, failing to get off at the right place on an island, because the name of our destination was not pronounced as we expected. When the crew realized what had happened, they immediately checked with the captain. They returned to tell us that the captain had agreed to go around the island again to let us off at the right dock. Soon the other passengers, mostly Malaysians, heard about our plight and expressed sympathy. And as they disembarked at the final official stop, several Muslim ladies in head scarves insisted on giving us bottles of water and snacks. After that, we got a private tour around the island, and the crew refused to take any money for it. Without our mistake, we would never have experienced that remarkable generosity, a highlight of our trip.

Is travel dangerous?

Nervous Nellies will have you fear everything about travel. But the risks are greatly exaggerated. An article in *Time* magazine, "How Americans Die Abroad" (March 8, 2016), noted that "On average, over the last 13 years, only 827 Americans died of unnatural causes while abroad each year." Compare that to the millions who traveled — 68 million in 2014 alone, according to the article. Traffic accidents are the most common cause of deaths of Americans abroad, with more than 3,000 killed between October 2002 and June 2015. (And you can do things to minimize that risk by driving safely and using seatbelts when available.)

What's more, in 2014 alone, the Centers for Disease Control and Prevention (CDC) stated that more than 31,000 deaths in the United States were caused by falls. In fact, if you're an American, your life-time odds of dying in an airplane accident are 1 in 96,566, while your odds of dying from a fall are 1 in 144. My conclusion? You could stay home to avoid the dangers of travel and die from a fall in your bath-tub or down your own front steps!

Today, terrorism is a very real threat. But, sadly, terrorist events can happen anywhere, and in the United States, which leads the world in gun deaths, you're not necessarily safer at home. According to a *CNN* article of December 30, 2015, for every American death caused by terrorism between 2001 and 2013 anywhere in the world, a thousand more were killed by guns here at home. (Statistics include accidental shootings and suicides.) In most places overseas, the biggest danger you will face is not for your personal safety, but for the loss of your personal items through pickpocketing or other theft.

You can check out the US State Department website to view travel advisories for specific areas. However, I think that the US site is likely to overstate risks somewhat. (We Americans are nervous people, and the government does not want to be criticized.) I often prefer to check the travel advisories on the Canadian, British, and Australian sites, because I believe their warnings are often more realistic. (Search "Travel advisories" and specify "US, Canadian, or UK government" to find the alerts.)

Remember, your overall odds of dying are 1 in 1. You won't get out of this world alive, so why not see more of it and enjoy it while you can?

Check out these tips to make your planning count.

Now that you've decided to go, here are some ideas to plan your trip successfully.

Keep it slow. Make the most of your time.

As an active senior, I'm sometimes reluctant to admit, even to myself, that travel can be tiring. But even if you want to visit several countries or areas, you will travel happier — healthier — if you don't rush. When I've become ill while traveling, it's usually because I have been pushing myself too hard.

One way of slowing down is to rent an apartment or cottage as a home base for a week or so, or do a home swap (covered in chapter 3). Your daily costs will also likely be much less than if you stay in a hotel or bed-and-breakfast (B&B). You can use your "home away from home" as a jumping-off spot for tours in the area. What works well with this strategy is that if you do find yourself tiring, you can take the day off. Just read, relax, or explore the area close to your rental. Having a chance to rejuvenate may be all you need.

Determine the length of your trip and your budget.

The length of your trip may well be determined by where you go and what you want to do. Long-term travel on a budget does require sacrifices. You must pick and choose the sights you will see, because you can't do it all.

You don't have to write off all the big, expensive cities of the world — that would be a mistake — but you can often save money by renting long term and, in areas with inexpensive public transportation, by staying outside of the city center.

To tour or not to tour?

There's nothing wrong with taking an organized tour if you can afford it. I am not disparaging tours. Often taking a tour will give you a richer background on the sights you view, so you can get more out of your trip. If you lack the time to plan or prepare, or if you're anxious about traveling on your own, a tour may be just what you want, especially if you're going abroad for the first time. A tour may provide a discount on high-end accommodations, compared to what you can book on your own, but if you are reading this book, you are probably not seeking an expensive trip. You can almost always travel longer and spend less by going on your own, if you don't require four-star travel.

If you decide to take a tour, it's still a good idea to research the destinations on your own to make sure the tour gives you enough time at the locations you most want to see. For example, some tours to Jordan spend only one day in Petra, the ancient "Rose City" carved into the red cliffs of stone. If you want more time to explore, you'll want to choose a tour that gives you two days to investigate this world treasure. Then check review sites such as *TripAdvisor* (***www.tripadvisor.com***) to see what others have to say about the tour company.

Still unsure about your tour operator? Members of USTOA (United States Tour Operators Association) are required to show some type of financial bonding, which can give you some assurance. In the UK, if you book with a tour group that is a member of ABTA (Association of British Travel Agents) your tour is protected financially in the event of the tour company's failure. Still, it is always a good idea to research a potential tour thoroughly. (See the Appendix for information on special tours.)

Should you take a cruise?

If you are considering taking a cruise, see chapter 4. For some people, especially those with serious mobility issues, a cruise can be a bargain, but you'll probably have to settle for a shorter time away, because long cruises are expensive.

Stay longer and rent outside of the city center.

Prices are lower outside of the tourist zone, and the less you move around and require expensive transportation, the more you'll save. You'll also experience more by becoming a temporary resident than by simply treading along to the same old tourist haunts. (Just make sure that public transportation in the area you are considering is not so expensive that it eats up all of your savings.)

How we saved euros, and became part of the neighborhood.

A few years ago, my husband and I spent nearly three months in Paris. Because we had friends and family coming to visit while we were there, we rented a two-bedroom apartment in a non-touristy neighborhood in Montmartre, which gave us the added benefits of friendly interactions with the local shopkeepers and other residents. One woman at our local bakery even cried and embraced me when I gave her a note to thank her for her kindness — a note written with help from Google Translate, since I speak little French and she spoke no English. My husband was even asked to mind a shop for a storekeeper while he ran an errand. Those encounters would have been less likely in the highly touristed city center.

Best of all, our lodging, meals, sightseeing, and transportation in the city (by Metro) cost less for the two of us on our two-and-a-half-month trip than most two-week tours of France from tour companies. (In both cases, that's exclusive of airfare, but our airfare was covered by frequent-flier miles in any case.)

How much will your trip cost?

Determining how much your trip will cost is perhaps the hardest part of planning a trip. Exchange rates and prices change often. By the time guidebooks are published, their prices are often out of date and the costs of accommodations listed in those books are frequently higher, sometimes because the economy has changed and sometimes because the owners get a little greedy when they are listed in a major guide.

Asking how much a trip around the world, or even a stay in one country, will cost is a little like asking, "What does a car cost?" It's possible to get a reliable car that runs for $3,000 — it may not have all the gadgets or look stylish, but you could do it — or you could spend $200,000 or more for a Lamborghini. Your style of travel will determine your costs more than anything else.

AirTreks (**www.airtreks.com**), a company that arranges round-the-world (RTW) tickets, states on its website that the cost will be between $20,000 and $30,000 a year per person. But those costs can vary considerably. Where you go, when you go (peak or off-season), and how you go all affect that price. That seems like a reasonable cost to me, based on how we traveled on our RTW trip in 2015–2016. You may prefer to travel a bit more upscale or a little more on the frugal side. However, remember that price *includes the normal daily living expenses* that you would have at home — such as food, transport, and utilities — so it's not an extra $20,000 to $30,000 per person.

On our RTW trip, we held ourselves to an average of $140–$150 per day for food, lodging, and local transport for both of us and usually spent closer to the lower figure. That number does not include airfare, a few of our car rentals, or the cost of our travel health insurance. Those numbers reflect a daily *average*. We spent more in some locales and far less in others. Interestingly, we had more trouble sticking to that budget in the two months we toured the Western United States than we did anywhere abroad. We found better budget lodging options elsewhere.

For that price overseas, we stayed in clean, attractive apartments. They were typically mid-scale and not luxurious, though some had amazing views and features. We mostly ate in our apartment or picnicked. Instead of eating at restaurants, we treated ourselves to coffee or a drink at a bar or cafe with a nice view or where we could people-watch. Only occasionally did we eat out. In cheaper places, like Budapest, we indulged ourselves with restaurant meals more often, but at neighborhood places, not at the ones with three Michelin stars. (We sometimes wished we could have sampled more fine restaurants, but that was a sacrifice we were willing to make. After all, nothing prevented us from savoring the delicious bread and pastries from traditional bakeries or delicacies and wine from local markets.) We occasionally rented a car, but we mostly used public transportation.

Again, you can lower your cost if you choose options such as a home exchange, a stay with friends, a volunteer vacation, or a hospitality service. If you don't mind using hostels or staying in a rented room, your costs will probably be lower still. (Full disclosure: In some places, we stayed with friends or shared expenses, which helped our budget immensely.)

Matt Kepnes, who is an author and blogger known as Nomadic Matt (**www.nomadicmatt.com**), wrote the book *How to Travel the World on $50 a Day or Less*. Though Matt targets a younger demographic, his book and website can be a valuable resource for seniors who want to price their travels and to reduce costs while on the go.

Get familiar with websites that help you estimate costs.

Most of us tailor our trips to what a budget can allow. If you're hesitant, you can use the websites below to estimate what lodging and other items cost at your chosen locales. Bookmark the ones you like, because you will return to them later when you're ready to make your arrangements. (You'll find more in-depth information on transportation in chapter 2 and on lodging in chapter 3.)

Determine the costs of lodging and airfare.

Airbnb (**www.airbnb.com**) offers a range of accommodations. Check a given city to see what you can get in a particular price range, taking care to note the additional fees (such as cleaning costs) to see the price of a particular type of rental. On Airbnb, you can rent a shared space, a private room, or an entire house or apartment. Remember, at this point, you're not going to book but are simply checking the range of prices.

Check out *AARP Expedia* (**www.expedia-aarp.com**) for hotels, bed-and-breakfasts (B&Bs), car rentals, and flights. Not a member of *AARP* (**www.aarp.org**)? It might be time to sign up, because it offers additional discounts and benefits. However, many times hotels will offer senior discounts of 10 to 15 percent even without an AARP membership — but you usually have to ask, so don't forget.

Take a look at *Booking.com* (**www.booking.com**) as well. I have not used *Kayak* (**www.kayak.com**) or *Trivago* (**www.trivago.com**) extensively, but those sites, which search multiple travel websites, can save you time. However, when you actually get ready to book a hotel or airfare, it's always a good idea to check the actual hotel or airline website too. Sometimes they will offer the same or a lower price, and it's easier to make changes and adjustments through the hotel or carrier than through a booking service.

Another resource, *Hostel World* (**www.hostelworld.com**), receives high recommendations for both hostels and low-budget hotels. (And yes, some hostels today offer private rooms and attached bathrooms, or ensuites, and will accept older travelers.)

See *Skyscanner* (**www.skyscanner.com**) for estimates on flights, especially intra-Europe flights. Know that the price can change depending on season. I like Skyscanner because, unlike the more well-known booking sites, it includes the smaller budget carriers. It sometimes makes sense to fly to a gateway city in Europe (for example, Dublin or London), then book a flight on a discount airline to your desired destination.

Another site that is often recommended in travel articles for flights and hotels abroad is *Momondo* (**www.momondo.com**). For hotels and flights in Asia, *Zuji* (**www.zuji.com**) sometimes has bargains that don't appear on US or Canadian sites. And if you plan to go to multiple countries on more than one continent, check out round-the-world (RTW) or regional airfares.

You should now have a very rough idea of lodging at your chosen locales and the approximate costs of getting from place to place. (Again, bookmark these sites for later reference.) These initial steps are meant only to give you an idea of daily costs and transportation within a region, but not necessarily all of your airfare costs. (You'll find information on cruises and freighters in chapter 2 in addition to other transport, but to simplify the initial planning, we'll assume you're not going to take a boat across an ocean. You can always take a look at that later.)

Compare the cost of living at home and abroad.

What will it actually cost to live, on a day-to-day basis, where you are going? *Numbeo* (**www.numbeo.com**) is a useful website for comparing costs in various cities around the world. It's not 100 percent accurate, but it can give you a "ballpark" idea. You can compare prices in your home city with any city in the world. Numbeo looks at groceries, rent, typical restaurant prices, and more to provide insights into the cost of living. (When planning a trip to France, I was delighted to find out that although many things cost more in Paris, wine, cheese, and baguettes were much cheaper! What more do you need?)

You'll also find *BootsnAll* (**www.bootsnall.com**), a website that caters to independent travelers, a valuable resource. Of course, you need not check all the above-listed sites every time you want to make a booking. But if you check them out, you'll probably find one or two that you like the most or that deliver the best values for you over time.

Review these recommendations for initial trip planning:

After you have picked the places you want to go and have a tentative daily budget, here are some additional tips:

- Create a spreadsheet or listing of what it costs to live in your home now. Make a separate list of the costs that you'll have even when you're on the road. When we did this exercise before our RTW trip, we found that even if we rented our condo, there were many expenses that we couldn't shed. We had to keep paying our Medicare premiums and insurance costs (Medicare supplement, life, condo, and car), taxes, and condo association fees. It was more than we initially expected.

- We then adjusted the amount we thought we could safely take from our savings. In that situation, you may decide to shorten your trip, to sell certain items, or perhaps to work longer or part-time, until you're better able to manage financially. Or maybe you'll decide to change your style of travel. In any case, having this information is vital to planning.

After you know which expenses you absolutely cannot cut, you can figure out your trip costs and how much extra money you need. To begin:

- Get a sheet of lined paper or use a computer spreadsheet. Create two columns. In the first column, write your dates, including the day of the week, such as "Monday, June 1." Then write the place you intend to stay beside each date. Alternatively (and this is what I usually do), print out free online calendar sheets and fill in the dates. Write in pencil or make more than one copy, so you can make changes. Calendar sheets have the advantage of making it easier to visualize a month at a glance. If you find you're trying to do too much, you can make adjustments.

- For a multi-month trip, you may want to start first by determining which places you will go to within a specific month, before you write down all the individual dates. If you have the broad outlines, you can fill the rest in as you travel. But at least get an idea of the costs at each of the places you intend to visit.

- Use the website *Rome2Rio* (***www.rome2rio.com***) to check whether your itinerary is doable. Rome2Rio is very good at showing you transport options between cities, how long each option takes, and how much it costs. Although you'll need to double-check the websites for the various means of transport before you book — especially because costs can rise — Rome2Rio offers a good tool to see how practical your itinerary is for both time and money. One caveat: Rome2Rio is not 100 percent accurate and sometimes misses possible connections. If you're searching a specific mode of transportation (for example, train or airline travel), check rail maps for the country or region you want to travel through to view the possible routes. Just do a web search naming the country or region and "rail map." Use Skyscanner (***www.skyscanner.com***) to confirm which airlines fly to your destination.

- Your earlier research on tours can provide a rough idea of how much time it will take to move from spot to spot, but remember tour groups can travel much faster, because someone else has made all the arrangements for restaurants, hotels, and tourist sites. Traveling on your own, you'll want to build in extra time. However, the biggest complaint I have heard from senior friends who take tours is that the schedules can be brutal. On a tour, you may have to rise before dawn and travel hours by bus before you get to the next location. As an independent traveler, for the most part, you don't have to do that, unless you want to get up early to get a bargain on an early-morning flight.

If you're traveling to several places, allow yourself an absolute minimum of two to three full days in each location, and plan longer stretches in between. (Trust me, that's better than wearing yourself out trying to see everything.) Remember, your goal is to go slow and enjoy your travels. But, when you do a review of your itinerary, be sure to check which days of the week the sights that you want to see are open, so you don't miss something critical.

Regardless of how you plan, take advantage of your independent travel style to savor each place you visit. You will get a much better feel of the daily vibe of a city than someone who simply passes through on an organized tour. You will become a real, if temporary, resident.

Use travel hacking to stretch your money.

Travel hacking — finding ways to increase your frequent flier miles or points for free airline tickets or hotel stays — is an art in itself, but you don't have to get too creative to benefit from the points-or-miles game.

Matt Kepnes of the Nomadic Matt blog is the author of *The Ultimate Guide to Travel Hacking*, and there are others. I once took a class on travel hacking from a Seattle-area woman who took several nearly free trips while still a graduate student. (I say "nearly free," because you will have to pay taxes and airport fees, even with frequent flier miles.) I am not like George Clooney's character in "Up in the Air," who never does anything unless it yields him miles, but I still do my share of tapping my credit card to earn miles. I have a friend who even charges her groceries on her credit card to rack up miles. She usually pays the economy fare and uses her miles to upgrade to business class, although that is becoming more difficult.

True travel hackers sign up for credit cards that offer thousands of miles as signing bonuses. Most of these offers require you to charge a specific amount within a given time — typically, you must charge $3,000 to $4,000 in the first few months. The credit card industry has tightened the rules somewhat, so it's not as easy to get these bonuses as it once was. However, if you sign up for a card (usually free the first year), get the bonus, and then cancel right before the year's end, you could then sign up for another without any problem, but with one big caveat: you must maintain a good credit score.

The only way for travel hacking to work (even if you use such techniques infrequently) is if you're absolutely certain you'll pay off your credit card each month, so that you never accrue interest! If you have ever had trouble with credit, *do not* take that route! Don't fool yourself — this time won't be any different. There is a reason that the British call buying on credit "the never-never." And if you're a senior on a limited income, you can't afford to take any chances on unending debt.

Check out the best credit cards for travel in chapter 4. Also, you may want to get a card that offers points rather than miles (see cards offered by Chase or American Express) now that airlines are awarding miles on the basis of ticket costs rather than by miles flown. Points can be assigned to various airlines and allow flights without blackout dates and with fewer restrictions. However, many cards that offer points will also have high annual fees, so research carefully. Points can also be exchanged for hotel bookings.

After you have an approximate idea of the daily costs of your trip and a tentative itinerary, it's time to make adjustments and start your preparations. First, consider passport and visa requirements, and then you can get closer to nailing down your airfare.

Please note that the information on passports applies to US citizens only. Citizens of other countries can check with the appropriate passport agency in their countries.

Get your passport — or check now to see if it's still valid.

Allow plenty of time to arrange for a passport or ensure that your current one is up-to-date. Many countries require that your passport is valid not only for the length of your trip but also for at least three months after the ticketed date of your return.

A US passport is good for ten years and, as of the time of this writing, costs $135. You can apply or renew online or make an appointment at a passport agency. You will find good information, and an application, at the US Department of State website: ***https://travel.state.gov/content/passports/en/passports.html***. (Or simply search the web for "US Passport.")

If you're applying for a passport for the first time, you must apply in person, but you can download the application from the State Department website. Check the website for the documents you need to apply and the requirements for the passport size photo that you must submit. (See "First Time Applicants" under the "Before You Go" tab on the State Department site.)

It usually takes about six weeks to get your passport, although you can pay extra to have it expedited. But why not avoid the stress and get it early? Having your passport in hand can lift your spirits, too, because it makes your dream trip seem so much closer.

Do you need a visa in advance of your arrival?

US citizens are fortunate. We can visit many countries without obtaining a visa in advance. A helpful site for checking whether you need a visa, regardless of your citizenship, is the *International Air Transport Association (IATA) Travel Centre* website (*www.iatatravelcentre.com*). It not only provides information on visas but also on whether particular vaccinations are advised for the country/countries you plan to visit. (It's always a good idea to double-check each country's own website too, because requirements can change.) US citizens can also find that information by doing a web search on "US State Department" and then clicking on "Country Specific Information." It's good to know if you need a visa for a particular country, because you often must apply far ahead of time. If you have to mail your passport to the nearest consulate to get your visa, you may be without it for several weeks.

Some countries make it easy for you to get a visa online. Australia allows that, for example, although the odd thing is that the Australian authorities never give you an actual stamp or piece of paper — they simply associate your visa with your passport number. Save your email correspondence, just in case something goes wrong.

If Europe is your destination, you might think all countries in the European Union (EU) have the same visa requirements, but that's not true. Even before the United Kingdom (UK) voted to leave the EU, an American could stay six months in the UK without a special visa. However, a US citizen can spend only a total of 90 days in most of the rest of Europe, in the countries that are bound by the Schengen Agreement, which include: Austria, Belgium, Czech Republic, Denmark, Estonia, Finland, France, Germany, Greece, Hungary, Iceland, Italy, Latvia, Liechtenstein, Lithuania, Luxembourg, Malta,

Netherlands, Norway, Poland, Portugal, Slovakia, Slovenia, Spain, Sweden, and Switzerland.

The following European countries are not currently part of the Schengen area: Bulgaria, Croatia, Cyprus, Ireland, Romania, and the United Kingdom, but check the current status for those countries before you go.

While you can stay just 90 days out of 180 *total* in all of the Schengen countries, *you can still stay (legally) for more than a year in Europe*. In addition to the six months you're allowed by the UK, the Republic of Ireland allows Americans to stay 90 days within its borders without a special visa.

So how do you stay more than a year? Simple. Do the "Schengen shuffle."

Take advantage of the "Schengen shuffle."

If you spend your first three months in the Republic of Ireland, then spend six months in the UK, and go on to the European continent for another three months, you have completed a year. (Of course, you could also go to the Schengen countries on the continent first). The critical thing is that you must stay out of the Schengen countries for 90 days* before you return. Then, if you like, you can repeat the process.

You can go back and forth from the Schengen area, but you have to keep within the 90 days in 180. That is, you can't restart the clock by exiting the area and returning in a day or so. You must abide by the requirements of each country or area. In no case overstay your visa.

Make your initial planning checklist.

To summarize, if your initial planning is complete, you will have:

- ☐ Visited the library to get books and magazines that feature the places you would like to experience.

- ☐ Used the resources cited above to get an idea of lodging, airfare, and living costs in the cities or areas that you want to visit.

- ☐ Calculated how many days you will stay at each place, based on the time and budget available with either a spreadsheet, paper, and/or calendar pages.

- ☐ Adjusted your itinerary and checked out *Rome2Rio* to see if you have allowed enough time to get between your destinations and (roughly) how much traveling between locations will cost.

- ☐ Ensured that your must-sees are open on the dates you will be in a specific city.

- ☐ Checked to make sure your passport is valid and have identified the visas you will need, if any.

Remember, this is just your tentative daily budget and itinerary. You'll be adjusting as you go. In fact, you should allow an extra 15 percent in your budget for unexpected costs. In the next chapters, we will talk further about options that can help you refine your planning.

Note: If your desire is to stay more than one year in one country, you'll need to check with the official government website of that country. Rules for long-stay visas vary considerably from country to country, and the restrictions can be tight. Typically, you'll have to show you have the funds to support yourself without working, and you will need to demonstrate you have valid medical insurance, so you won't be a burden on the country. (Medical insurance is not required in Mexico and in some other Latin American countries.)

CHAPTER 2:

TRANSPORTATION — HOW WILL YOU GET AROUND?

Subways and trams, like this one in Budapest, make city travel easy.

How will you get to your first destination? How will you travel after that? Most independent travelers who cross an ocean go by air, but your travel will most likely involve a combination of transportation modes.

Airline pricing is a mystery.

Have you ever felt that airlines price their flights in some back room where employees either throw darts at a board or make up creative combinations such as "if it's a full moon and the red crabs are migrating" then we will increase the fare 200 percent? You could be forgiven for thinking that! Passengers on the same flight sitting right next to one another can pay vastly different prices for their seats — so you need all the help you can get.

When should you book award tickets?

While it's more difficult to use frequent flier miles now than in the past, they still represent a great bargain, and some airlines now make it easier to discover when award seats are available by displaying award charts that show availability on all dates during a given period.

I've had good luck finding mileage flights (knock on wood!) by booking far in advance. Airline reservation systems display flights up to 330 days in advance of travel, and that can be a promising time to book. Because most people book flights 30 to 90 days prior to travel, availability is often good from about 11 months to 3 or 4 months prior to travel — but finding mileage award flights gets more difficult at the last minute.

ExpertFlyer (**www.expertflyer.com**) can be a helpful site to search for award flights. Its basic subscription is $4.99 month, which allows you to set up alerts to notify you when a seat becomes available on the date you wish to fly. However, you don't need a subscription to set free alerts. (Check out "New to ExpertFlyer" at the top of the home page if you haven't used the site before.)

Save on regular airline fares.

Today, in some parts of the world, including Europe, Asia, and New Zealand/Australia, you can often find big savings by flying on budget airlines such as *Easyjet* and *Ryanair* (Europe) and *Tiger Air* and *Air Asia* (New Zealand/Australia and Asia). You can often save hundreds of dollars by flying with a major airline to your first destination and taking budget airlines to other countries in the region. (See **www.easyjet.com**, **www.ryanair.com, www.tigerair.com**, and **www.airasia.com**.)

If you have an Alaska Airlines credit card, you can also put this strategy to work by using your Alaska companion fare to fly to a US city that offers a better fare to the region you want to fly to. (Or, of course, use miles from any airline credit card to get there.)

Sometimes you can also get free stopovers to extend your trip. For example, as of this writing, *Icelandair* (**www.icelandair.com**) offers a free stopover in Iceland when traveling from the United States or Canada to Europe. You can stay in Iceland for up to seven nights at no additional airfare. The airline even offers free "stopover buddies," pairing you with an Icelandair employee who will act as your host for one day, during the slower winter season. (No guarantees this offer will last however.)

Alaska Airlines (**www.alaskaair.com**) has a helpful primer on its blog on how to get a free stopover on its partner airlines. Just go to **https://blog.alaskaair.com/alaska-airlines/mileage-plan/international-stopovers/**.

Consider open-jaw flights and combinations.

Don't overlook flying "open-jaw," arriving in one city and leaving from another. While open-jaw tickets are almost always more expensive than round-trip tickets, you can often save money (and time) because you do not need to return to your original arrival city. (Check the "multi-city" or "multiple destinations" button on the search engine to review flights.)

If you plan to use a major airline for your longest flights and book seats on budget airlines within regions, remember to consider the cost of baggage. Discount airlines — and today, even many larger carriers — make money by selling extras, including baggage fees and early boarding. On some airlines, the limits are so strict you can only carry a purse or briefcase as a carry-on, so you're forced to check even a small bag, often at a steep cost. Read the disclosures on the web site very carefully. Also, you should know that many of the budget airlines fly from smaller airports that are sometimes a long way from the cities they serve, so check the airport locations and transportation options too.

Given the fees, and the sometimes inconvenient airports of the discount carriers, you may actually find it as cheap to fly on a mainstream airline. But it's definitely worth checking your options. Budget airlines may not offer all the creature comforts, but they must adhere to the same strict safety standards as other airlines.

Search more than one site.

I usually do my initial searches for airfares on *Skyscanner* (**www.skyscanner.com**). I like the fact that the site includes budget airlines in its search, which some of the larger travel search websites do not. Skyscanner includes a calendar that can show the cheapest fares in a month and offers to send you alerts when your airfare changes. (To see prices for an entire month, enter the travel dates for your departure and arrival cities, click "Search flights," and then click "Show whole month" on the page where flights are displayed.)

Another site, *Kayak* (***www.kayak.com***), also scans multiple airline prices, as does *Hopper*, a free mobile app for your tablet or smartphone. Hopper offers a view-at-a-glance interface that shows the cheapest dates to fly. It also provides predictions on whether your fare will rise or fall, when, and by how much, based on historical rates. But perhaps the best feature of Hopper is its *Fair Bear* feature. Now that airlines want to charge extra for everything (sometimes including blankets!) and are offering extremely basic fares that give passengers nothing but a cramped seat, Fair Bear makes it easy to see the real costs of your airline fare. It advises you about each airline's fees, such as those for seat selection or changes and cancellations, as well as carry-on allowances, so it's easier to make comparisons.

After you have found a good fare, go to the website of the airline itself, because you may find a better price through a sale. On foreign carriers, you can also see if the airfare is cheaper when booked in another currency. You can book in that currency and still use your US or Canadian credit card, but make sure it has no foreign transaction fees. Here are some other good search sites for airfare:

Expedia: ***www.expedia-aarp.com***

Booking.com: ***www.booking.com***

Momondo: ***www.momondo.com*** (for international fares; you may have to enter the address manually)

Zuji: ***www.zuji.com*** (for fares in Asia)

What's more, you can still shop for deals on *Priceline* (***www.priceline.com***), but the "name your own price" feature for airline tickets ended in 2016.

Scott's Cheap Flights offers another option.

Recently, I learned about *Scott's Cheap Flights* (**www. scottscheapflights.com**), a service that I've not yet tried, but it sounds like it may offer some real possibilities, particularly for those who can prepare to leave quickly or are flexible on their dates. Scott's advertises airline sales fares for international travel or — for even more savings — fares that airlines post by mistake (such as listing a $800 flight for $8.00). Offering both a paid and free service, giving paid subscribers more specials and first notice, Scott's advises consumers to check the airline's own website immediately, because many of the fares disappear almost at once, especially those posted in error.

What is the best time to book? Any time!

Although some experts will tell you that Tuesday at 3 p.m. Eastern Time (US) is when airlines typically create fare sales, that's not a solid rule. If you're traveling internationally, it's a good idea to book your tickets five or six months in advance — and even further out if you are trying to use air miles.

Weigh savings against comfort.

When you're traveling on a tight budget, it's hard to make air travel very comfortable! Kevin and I often travel in what we call "steerage" (a.k.a., economy). You can use miles to upgrade (if you have them), or pay an extra fee to fly in the enhanced economy section, Economy Plus (on United) and Economy Comfort (on Delta), for example. We will sometimes pay the extra fee for flights when we want to try to sleep, because we get a little more room. But often it's a price we just don't want to pay. It's hard enough to stay within our budget. You can check out *Seatguru* (**www.seatguru.com**) to view seat maps for specific planes.

Do you want to play the odds at 20,000 feet?

While it's not something I would count on, some of the savviest travelers try to book bulkhead seats — the ones located directly behind the partitions separating passengers from the galley or toilets. Given that airlines now often charge extra for exit-row seats — the other economy seats that offer more legroom — snagging a bulkhead seat can be quite a perk. You need to check Seatguru, though, because some bulkhead seats are roomier than others. And because airlines often include space for bassinets at those seats, you could find yourself seated next to a fussy, crying passenger (the mom or dad?).

However, using strategy may pay off. For example, if there are three bulkhead seats with only the aisle seat taken, it might be worth the gamble. Most people don't travel alone with babies if they can help it, so an occupied aisle seat may represent a single adult.

Another ploy that some people use is to reserve a middle seat in a middle row, if it's close to the departure day and the flight isn't full. They figure that outside seats will be reserved first, and by sitting in the middle, they'll have a good chance to spread out. Of course, there are no guarantees. But your chances are better than winning the lotto!

Here's my personal rant for more room!

Recently, there have been several incidents of travelers squabbling (and even coming to blows) over trays that recline into passengers' heads and devices that defend knee space. But here's the thing — this is entirely prevent-able! Instead of blaming each other, we should be writing letters to the airlines and our congressional representatives complaining about squeezing us into seats designed to fit a third-grader and insisting on reasonable room!

Make the most of RTW tickets.

While you can piece together your own tickets for a round-the-world (RTW) journey, I think most of us are happy to have help. When Kevin and I made our RTW trip, we used a combination of tickets, some booked with frequent-flier miles and some with discount airlines, as well as an RTW fare. (We used frequent flier miles to travel to and from Europe, then booked the RTW fare on Air New Zealand—a fare not available in the US— out of London, because we planned to spend the summer in England before returning to the United States.)

The Air New Zealand RTW tickets gave us a free stopover on the way to New Zealand (which we used to return to the US for Christmas), and a free stopover on the way back (Singapore). We used both discount airlines and major carriers within New Zealand and Australia. Our RTW tickets took us to Singapore, but we knew several budget airlines fly from there, so we planned to fly to other parts of Asia on discount airlines. Because Air New Zealand is a member of the Star Alliance, we earned miles on the RTW tickets that we could use later with United Airlines, and some of the other carriers that we used also had partnerships that earned us air miles.

Booking RTW tickets can be complicated, so I gladly paid a $50 fee to have an Air New Zealand representative help me plan our itinerary. In 2015, our RTW tickets cost us $2,750 each, although we spent about another $1,200 each on budget flights.

Tap the benefits of the alliances.

There are three major airline alliances that offer RTW fares: the *Star Alliance, Oneworld,* and *SkyTeam.* Rules for the RTW fares differ by the alliance. For example, Star Alliance and SkyTeam RTW tickets are based on the number of miles traveled, while Oneworld offers a choice of a continent-based fare or a distance-based fare. Usually, fares are valid for one year and you need to begin and end your travels in the same country. Depending on your itinerary, an RTW fare can be a fantastic bargain and offer valuable flexibility. Our RTW ticket through *Star Alliance,* for example, charged for changes in destination but not for switching dates — a big advantage when we unexpectedly had to return home early. (If you need to make changes to your RTW ticket, you have to call the airline that you initially made the booking with.)

Check out the rules for RTW tickets on each of the alliance sites. You can even build in a possible itinerary and view the associated costs. Wikitravel offers a good review of the various alliance RTW fares and discusses the coverage of each. (Search for Wikitravel and "round the world flights.") Here are the websites for the three main alliances:

> *Star Alliance:* **www.staralliance.com**
> *Oneworld:* **www.oneworld.com**
> *SkyTeam:* **www.skyteam.com**

You can also book an RTW ticket with frequent flier miles.

Benefit from the expertise of RTW services.

Agencies that specialize in RTW tickets, such as *AirTreks* (***www.airtreks.com***), provide another option for arranging round-the-world travel. One advantage of AirTreks is that it can combine tickets from multiple airlines, which often lets them book cheaper fares. If you need to make a change, you can call them and they will make the change for you. They also let you travel some segments overland. Check out the AirTreks website to see sample itineraries and costs. Be sure before you book that you understand the costs of re-booking various segments should you need to make changes later.

Note: The transportation modes discussed below refer to traveling between cities or regions, not intracity travel.

Should you consider a cruise?

Few people cross an ocean by boat these days, and those who do usually spring for a cruise, which can add significantly to transportation costs. Generally, a cruise will be more expensive than other modes of travel. You will have to compare the cruise cost with airfare and your daily budget, so for most travelers a cruise is not an option for an ocean crossing or for moving from place to place. But for some people, such as those with mobility issues, it may be a reasonable choice.

One difficulty for budget travelers is that the heaviest discounts on cruises are typically at the last minute, making planning difficult for a multi-month trip. If you want to investigate a cruise, then take a look at these resources:

Cruise Sheet: (***https://cruisesheet.com***)

Cruise Deals: (***http://www.cruisedeals.com***)

Though I haven't used them myself, they are recommended by experts such as Matt Kepnes of the Nomadic Matt blog and by CNNMoney and USA Today. You may also find cruise travel specialists in your own city who can find good deals. Signing up for email notices at a cruise line can also net you a bargain, because you get advance notice of specials. In addition to traveling in the low season, you can get good buys on repositioning cruises (for example, when cruise lines move their ships from the east-coast ports of the United States to Southern Europe in the fall and back again in the spring). Find out more about cruising and check reviews at *Cruise Critic* (**www.cruisecritic.com**).

Freighter travel has lost its allure.

Travel by freighter, once tantalizingly romantic, is no longer an attractive option for most people. Today, with container cargo, time in port is extremely limited and quarters are cramped. Amenities are few, and many voyages are long, with days on end spent at sea. In addition, most freighters take only 12 passengers at a time. If that option still appeals to you, you can find more information on the Wikitravel website, including a list of agencies that specialize in freighter travel at ***http://wikitravel.org/en/Freighter_travel***.

Take the train and see the countryside.

When you're not crossing oceans, you can cover much of the earth by rail. A train journey is one of the most romantic ways to travel — unless of course, you're stuck in an older, dirty, rattle-trap of a carriage. Our first trip to Europe, over 30 years ago, involved a multi-week journey mostly taken by train with our trusty Eurail passes. Sadly, today rail passes are rarely a bargain, and discount airlines have made it much cheaper to travel by air throughout Europe.

Train travel in other parts of the world can vary from a near-luxury experience in a speedy bullet train to an only-to-be-endured experience. (I'm looking at you, Circumvesuviana, you dusty, pickpocket-prone train from Naples to Sorrento.)

Most of the time, you can easily buy train tickets in Europe at train stations, either from a clerk or from a ticket machine (most also display in English). You can usually save money if you book in advance, from weeks to three months prior to leaving. Get your tickets from US travel agencies (or at *www.ricksteves.com*) for a small fee, or buy them at other online sites. The English version of the German Rail (*Deutsche Bahn*) website is a reliable way to book tickets. (See *www.bahn.com*).

My favorite place to book trains in Europe is *Loco2* (*https://loco2.com*), a British site, but it doesn't cover as many countries as the German Rail site, as of this writing. If you book European trains on Loco2 and a seat reservation is required, you'll automatically be assigned a seat. The site is very easy to use. You will be given an electronic reservation number, which you can save on your smartphone or tablet, or simply write down the number and show it to the conductor. (I'd advise writing it down and keeping any emails in case of a problem.)

Loco2 also lists senior discounts for various European countries on its website, with links to the respective sites, and makes it easy to add a senior railcard number (see below) when booking.

If you plan a long stay in one country, it may pay to get a railpass or a railcard. While you can sometimes book senior fares without a railcard, some places require that you buy one first. (Make sure you have your passport to prove your age.) In the UK, for example, anyone over the age of 60 can buy a senior railcard for about £30 (about

$37 in early 2017), which provides a discount of one-third on your rail tickets. That investment can result in big savings if you are taking even a few train journeys, and the card is good for a year. (Several other countries, including Spain, also offer discount rail cards.)

For visits of a few weeks in one location, also look into possible discounts for transportation within the city. A little research can pay off. When we spent two-and-a-half months in Paris a few years ago, we bought monthly Metro passes that not only saved us on our trips around town, but also allowed us to travel free anywhere in the Île-de-France region on summer weekends. I'm not sure if that option is still offered, but it never hurts to investigate.

In some parts of the world, train travel is very expensive. In Europe, if you are traveling a long distance, you can probably do better to fly or take a bus. Train travel is also expensive in Australia. If you are interested in train travel anywhere in the world, get some inside tips from *The Man in Seat 61* (**www.seat61.com**).

Buses are often a cheap and comfortable way to go.

Bus travel usually costs less than going the same distance by train. However, the quality of the coaches varies widely, even within a single country. Buses in less affluent countries can be surprisingly better than in the United States. For example, the intercity buses in Turkey are quite pleasant and are often air-conditioned, although the drivers may not always turn it on. (Locals are used to the heat. In Mediterranean countries, don't be surprised if you see people wearing wool clothing in the summer, when the tourists are garbed in T-shirts and shorts.) Many places in Mexico also have efficient, clean coaches between cities, and you may even have a seatback video screen. Kevin and I found the intercity buses in Morocco comfortable too.

It pays to research the bus service, because the notorious "chicken bus" (people and livestock) still exists in many parts of the world. It's sometimes the only way for local farmers to get to market. However, nothing makes for better travel stories, and you'll usually find people quite friendly and curious if you travel as the locals do.

In Europe, there are several long-distance budget bus companies, but they focus on a younger backpacker crowd. Seats are often somewhat cramped, though many offer Wi-Fi. On some routes, buses drive for hours non-stop, but others stop frequently, making the journeys quite long. (I have no personal experience with these long-distance buses.)

There is no denying the bargains, however. In 2016, Flixbus, a German company, introduced a €99 fare for bus journeys of up to five European cities within three months. With more than 900 destinations available, that's an incredible deal, as long as you know what to expect.

If you're interested in exploring inexpensive long-distance bus travel in Europe, however, here are some options:

> Flixbus: **www.flixbus.com**
>
> Eurolines: **www.eurolines.com**
>
> Megabus: **www.megabus.com**

Greyhound Australia (**www.greyhound.com.au**) is the only national bus company in that country, and it offers several different passes. But in both Australia and in New Zealand, with its *Kiwi Backpacker Experience* (**www.kiwiexperience.com**), long-distance bus services seem mostly designed with young people in mind.

Research car rentals to find the best bargain.

In places where public transportation is nonexistent or infrequent, you really need a car to see the sights of interest. The west coast of Ireland, for example, is difficult to cover well without a private car. Buses are typically few and far between. You should know, however, that Ireland is one of the countries that requires you to purchase additional insurance, even if your credit card covers car rentals overseas. (We found very good rates and received good service from *Conn's Ireland Car Rental*, formerly EasytourIreland (***www.connsirelandcarrental.com***). Conn's rents Hertz cars at lower rates than on the Hertz site, and their quotes are fully inclusive. There are no surprises, unlike some companies that fail to fully disclose additional charges before booking.

If you want to find the best price for a car rental, the search sites mentioned above are the first place to start. But also check the major car rental websites; you may stumble across a special. And don't forget to ask about discounts for members of AARP, AAA, or (perhaps) your college alumni association.

After checking the sites that search multiple car rental companies, do a web search on "budget car rental + [name of country]". That was how I found Conn's Ireland Car Rental. You can wait until you reach your destination to rent a car, but you almost always save money by booking in advance. Advance booking works especially well when car rental companies offer free cancellation. In Europe, check out companies like Sixt and Payless as well, which are not as well known in the United States, but are often quite competitive.

If you're a little bit brave, you can also explore the "rent-a-dent" and "rent-a-wreck" type of car rentals that you can find online. But be sure and check the reviews and find out if the rental company has support services throughout your driving area. We have occasionally rented from such companies, which typically have older model cars that are not in pristine condition, and have found them satisfactory for our purposes. The cars were actually relaxing to drive because we didn't worry about getting scratches on them.

Think carefully about the kind of car you want to rent. Are you able to drive a vehicle with a stick-shift? Even if you are, you may still want to get an automatic if you need to drive on the opposite side of the road from your home country, because you'll have to switch to your other hand to shift. However, you can expect to pay more for an automatic overseas.

A small car can be an advantage in countries with narrow roads. (Ask my husband who once piloted a large van packed with our entire family, grandkids included, on the narrow rural roads of Scotland!) If you aren't carrying other passengers, you may be able to get by with the smallest economy car — and save your cash (although it's good to have a trunk or a covered hatch to hide your luggage.) Many times, you'll get a free upgrade if you reserve an economy vehicle, because rental car companies do not keep a large stock of the smallest cars.

Booking for a longer period can save you money too. Surprisingly, sometimes it can be cheaper to rent for a week than for five days, for example. Many companies also recalculate to the higher daily rate if you bring the car back early, which makes no sense but it's true! You should also be aware that there is often a steep charge for one-way rentals.

Find out in advance about surcharges for seniors.

Of special concern to seniors is the fact that in certain countries, there is an age limit on car rentals or rental companies will charge you more above a specific age — at times as low as 65 but more often 70 or 75. Some companies will rent to customers older than 75, but there can be special requirements, so check ahead of time. (For example, the company may require you to be a regular driver who has been accident-free for five years, or it may ask for a letter from your doctor confirming that you are in good health.)

The critical thing is to ask before you rent, because this information is sometimes not included on car-rental websites. I remember sitting in a car-rental agency at London Heathrow a few years ago, when one unfortunate 70-year-old found out when he came to pick up his car that a surcharge would be imposed because of his age. It may seem unfair, but at least it's better to know in advance.

Bring your own GPS or Sat/Nav.

Kevin and I recommend that you travel with your own GPS unit (or Sat/Nav as the devices are called in Europe), if you have one. Most GPS units have maps available on chips or for download that cover other parts of the world for a price. They are cheaper than paying for a unit from the rental service, and because you know how your own device works, presumably driving abroad will be less stressful.

You can also use the mapping software on your smartphone (Google Maps or Apple Maps), but remember to cache your maps, directions, and locations while you're using Wi-Fi so you can use them offline. If not, the data charges will be staggering! Although a GPS device is no substitute for a map, we would not drive anywhere without both.

Sur la droite! Sur la gauche!

We sometimes joke that our GPS unit has saved our marriage! At a minimum, it has saved many arguments about which route to take when we are on the road. But a map is also essential, because a GPS device is not foolproof.

An example: While traveling in France, we wanted to visit the popular medieval city of Sarlat-la-Canéda, but by following our GPS we arrived in the pedestrian-only center of the city. A passerby helped us out, directing us to a street two blocks away, where we could exit. Unfortunately, it was

a festival day, and the way was blocked by a large crowd watching an acrobat. Kevin pulled the car up to a stop, and we just sat, watching the people admiring the performance. Nervous, we silently prayed for a policeman. We didn't care if we got a ticket; we just wanted to get out of the city. The minutes ticked by, the acrobat continued his headstands, twists, and turns, and there wasn't a gendarme in sight. Eventually, the crowd thinned, but only slightly. I popped out of the car, enjoining Kevin, "Let's get out of here!" Relying on my half-remembered French from many moons ago, I faced the crowd, directing them to the right, calling, "Désolé! Sur la droite! Sur la droite, si'l vous plaît!" ("Sorry. To the right! To the right, please!") Then, I suddenly realized I was pointing them to *my* right, which would be *their* left. I immediately switched my call to the left: "Sur la gauche! Sur la gauche, si'l vous plaît!" Amazingly, mothers, fathers, kids, and grandparents all moved as I directed. As I walked on gesturing, parting the crowd, Kevin, who was following in our rental car, inched along until he reached the steep street that was our exit. I quickly climbed back into the car, and he sped up the hill, roaring out onto the road. As Sarlat receded in our rear-view mirror, we laughed hysterically, pleased that we got away without hitting one pedestrian! But the next time we came to town, we parked on the outskirts and ignored our GPS.

Be prepared to pay high prices for gas/petrol/diesel in other parts of the world, although because the distances between sights are often short, it's surprising how far you can go without filling the tank. Renting a small car saves on fuel costs as well.

Know about car-rental insurance before you go.

When you rent cars overseas, most companies want you to purchase their insurance because the basic liability coverage that comes with a rental has a very high deductible. Usually, the law mandates a specific amount of coverage that rental companies must maintain, but they can charge you for the deductible. The insurance is called a collision damage waiver (CDW), loss damage waiver, or excess charges. (Though lately companies seem to add some other ill-defined charges as well.)

A CDW essentially waives the rental company's right to charge you for accident-related damages. In some locations, such as Italy and Ireland, the insurance is mandatory, but in most places it is optional. This insurance can add significantly to the cost of your rental, so it's important to decide how to deal with it before you are standing at the rental counter. Your options include the following:

- *Decline the coverage and use your credit-card insurance.* This approach works only if you are certain your credit card offers this coverage. Make sure before you leave home that you call your credit card company to find out what, if any, coverage they have. Also, you must then rent the car using the specific credit card that offers the coverage — and you must decline the rental company's insurance.

- Realize that you will have to pay for any damage with your credit card and be reimbursed later (which can take some time), so make sure you know what records (for example, accident reports, etc.) your credit card issuer will ask for should an accident occur. The rental company may also place a hold on your card for the amount of the deductible if you decline their coverage. If your available credit is high enough that may not matter, but if not, be sure you have another credit card with you, just in case.

- *Decline the coverage and purchase CDW insurance from a private issuer.* In the past, I located a company that provided collision insurance at a cheaper rate than the car rental agency, but sadly that company no longer seems to be in business. However, some travel insurance companies, such as *Travelguard,* will let you add rental car collision insurance to your travel insurance policy. It could be worth comparing the charges. (See chapter 4 for more on travel insurance.)

Purchase the car-rental company insurance. Given the hassles, many people simply decide to pay the often-exorbitant insurance rates the rental car companies charge, so they can drive away with peace of mind knowing they are covered. You can always decline the coverage and simply decide to pay any claims out of pocket if you need to.

If you will be renting a car in non-English speaking countries, it's a good idea to get an international driver's permit. You can purchase a permit at your nearest American Automobile Association (AAA) in the United States or at the Canadian Automobile Association in Canada. (You can also get one by mail.) You'll probably never need it, but if you're in an accident or are stopped by the police, the international license may help. Many countries require that your license be translated, which is covered by the multi-lingual permit.

Learn about other transportation choices.

Depending on where you are in the world, you may find other transportation modes that serve your purposes and save you money.

Rent a campervan.

When "down under," seniors may want to consider renting a campervan, a popular way of getting around New Zealand and Australia. We prefer to simply get a budget car rental and rent apartments and cottages. (Even hotel rooms in New Zealand often come with a kitchenette.) However, in remote areas, a campervan gives you more flexibility. Check out companies online by doing a web search for "campervans" in each country.

Go with the locals in a shared taxi.

Whether they are called dolmus (Turkey), city taxis (Morocco), or jitneys (various places), these shared taxi services operate mostly in the same way. They travel a standard route, often from a main city center to small villages. The cost is much less than a standard taxi, because you share a van or other vehicle with others. Typically, shared taxis do not have a time of departure, they leave when the vehicle is full. If you're in a hurry you can offer to pay for additional people, so the van can get underway. (For example, if a dolmus holds eight passengers and there are only five on board, you could agree to pay three fares — yours and two others' — to speed the departure.) Usually, that's still far less than your own taxi.

Set sail on a ferry.

Just as with bus travel, ferry services range from basic (and potentially unsafe) transport to fairly luxurious passages, so you need to do your research. Look online or ask other travelers. Sometimes services are cheaper at different times of the day as well.

Buy tickets at travel agencies.

While there are fewer and fewer travel agencies in the United States, there are still places in the world where they are fairly common and can be quite helpful. For example, when traveling in Greece, you can use agencies to buy packages that combine air or ferry travel and hotels. (An office may push package sales, because that's how they make their money, but they will still often let you purchase individual tickets.) London and Singapore have travel agencies where you can often find good package deals as well.

Get around easily in the city.

Most cities offer several options for transportation, ranging from subways to taxis and ride services. Some municipalities offer passes or tickets that work on all the local public transportation services.

Take the subway or metro.

In most of the world, subways or elevated trains provide a quick and convenient way to cross the city. (Note that in London, a subway is a passage under the street and not the underground rail.) It really pays to get to know the public transportation options in the cities you visit, and although buses are typically cheaper, the speed of metropolitan lines such as the London Underground ("the Tube"), the Paris Metro, the Singapore MRT, and others make this mode of transportation one of the best. In each city, you will want to research the cost of tickets and find out if a pass makes sense for you. Even if you don't get a pass, ask if there are senior discounts. Many times you don't need a pass to get a discount, just proof of age.

Buses and trams cover the cities.

City buses and streetcars (trams) remain an excellent value in most parts of the world. You don't need to speak the language to take the bus or tram, but you need to do enough research to know if you have to buy your ticket in advance (for example, from a newsstand). If the bus pulls up to your stop and you aren't sure if it goes to your destination, just say the name of the stop, questioningly. Though it's not always foolproof (pronunciation varies, even in English-speaking countries), usually the driver will either nod or wave you onboard, or tell you the number or name of the appropriate bus. Passengers waiting at a bus stop will usually be happy to help you too. Get in and sit down quickly (or hang on), because in most of the world the driver will not wait for you to get settled before he (usually a he) takes off.

Taxis are useful, but they are budget busters.

Taking a taxi is easy and comfortable, but if you take them often in expensive cities, your budget will be shot! If you're traveling in a place where the local language is in a different alphabet or uses unfamiliar characters, be sure to take a card from the front desk or copy down (from the website or from the owner), the name and address of your temporary residence. Then, if you get lost, you can always hail a cab to get back.

Make sure you know what the official taxis look like, or you could get picked up by a rogue driver.

Legitimate taxis should have a meter. You can also negotiate an agreement in advance on the fare to go to a specific place. (Even then, we have had to argue a time or two.) Although we have had good luck over the years, we have probably been ripped off more often by taxi drivers than by anyone else. On the other hand, it can also be a pleasant experience to talk to your driver and find out more about life in a particular city — most of them are not crooks and are trying very hard to make a living. In Asia, Africa, or the Middle East, you may also find that the taxis lack seat belts. Your driver will probably insist they are not necessary, because he is a "good driver."

Some places offer special types of taxis such as the three-wheeled tuk-tuks, golf-cart-like conveyances, or carriages. The ones that offer inexpensive transportation are used by locals. Otherwise, cute, highly decorated vehicles are designed for tourists and are priced accordingly.

Try Uber and Lyft.

You can now find Uber and Lyft in many places throughout the world. To use these taxi-like services, you'll need a smartphone that can connect to local networks, so you can use the apps. You can also request an accessible ride if you have a disability, although some locales are better equipped than others.

Choose carbon offsets for greener travel.

Carbon offset programs, initially very popular, have become less so in recent years because many were not transparent, and while they made travelers who purchased them feel better, they did not accomplish what they promised. But today, there are organizations that certify programs that support global standards, so it's easier to select programs that actually do some good.

While driving zero-emissions cars helps us travel more responsibly on land, airline travel is more challenging. According to an article in the *New York Times* ("Your Biggest Carbon Sin May Be Air Travel," January 26, 2013), a single flight from New York to Europe dumps 2–3 tons of carbon dioxide *per person* into the atmosphere. Given that severe impact, which carbon offset programs do the most to help lessen that effect?

The best advice is to check whether a program meets the Voluntary Gold Standard, Voluntary Carbon Standard, or Climate Action Reserve (CAR) certification. Kevin and I have used *Terrapass* (***www.terrapass.com***), which is one of the most recommended carbon offset providers. *Atmosfair* (***www.atmosfair.com***), a German company, also offers carbon offsets for cruises, which many companies do not. If you come across others that impress you, let us know at ***www.seniorbudgettravel.com***. (Full disclosure: I'm embarrassed to admit we haven't always traveled green, but with today's verifiable standards, we'll be more inclined to do so in the future.)

What's next?

If you have decided how you will get between your major destinations, check out the transportation prices on the appropriate websites and compare them with your initial planning estimates. Also do some spot checks on the public transportation costs in the cities or areas you plan to visit, so you can make adjustments to your plans, if necessary.

CHAPTER 3:

CHOOSING ACCOMMODATIONS

Accommodations in Morocco can be both elegant and low-cost.

Where you stay can make or break your budget. You can find the lowest airfare and cut costs by using local transportation, but if you regularly exceed your accommodation budget, it's just about impossible to get back on track.

The good news is that the choices for budget accommodations have never been better. There are some surprising choices that can help you stay within your allowance and still experience the best that a location has to offer.

Find free or nearly free accommodations.

There's no better price than free! On the other hand, free accommodation may not seem like such a bargain if you don't enjoy your hosts.

Stay with friends or relatives.

If you have friends or relatives who live abroad, visiting them can be the best of both worlds — an opportunity to get acquainted or reacquainted and to see life from a local's perspective. Of course, you'll want to be a considerate guest, limiting your time to a few days, unless you're absolutely certain your friend or relative will welcome a longer visit. It's also polite to offer to return the favor and host them at your own place later, if you can. And everyone appreciates a gift or dinner out in appreciation.

Check out hospitality organizations.

Organizations that promote personal interactions, such as *Servas* (*www.servas.org*), open up more opportunities to meet local people. Founded in 1949, Servas bills itself as a worldwide cooperative cultural exchange network dedicated to fostering peace, goodwill, and mutual respect. It's an independent, non-profit, non-political group. Membership, as of 2016, is $98 per year. Travelers are limited to a two-night's stay with one host, with some exceptions, though subscribers may book an unlimited number of stays for one year. Some hosts also offer space to families and people with disabilities.

In addition to (or instead of) lodging, some members will offer to meet up with visitors or share a meal with them.

Still a free spirit? Try Couchsurfing (www.couchsurfing.org).

Although most couchsurfers are young, there is no age limit, and there are some senior hosts. Besides, you're not an ageist, are you? Couchsurfers create profiles. If you find a prospective host who shares your interest, that could be a way of making a new friend. However, accommodations may literally be a couch. It's probably only for the truly adventurous senior traveler, but it is an option. As with rental sites, it's wise to read the references carefully.

See the world by volunteering.

If you're healthy, yearn to experience other cultures, and have always wanted to make a real difference in people's lives, why not consider the *Peace Corps*? The Peace Corps doesn't have an age limit, although many positions require a bachelor's degree. In addition to the two-year commitment, there are now shorter programs available for 3–12 months. To find out more, check out "Volunteering at 50 Plus," at *www.peacecorps.gov/volunteer/is-peace-corps-right-for-me/50plus/*.

Joyce Major, author of *Smiling at the World*, offers advice on finding volunteer vacations that fit your passion and don't charge exorbitant fees. Her website is *www.inexpensiveglobalvolunteering.com*. Major says that retirees have an advantage with some volunteer opportunities, because organizations like people who can make a commitment of a month or more. She has volunteered throughout the world on projects ranging from teaching English and working on archeological digs to taking care of animals. (Remember that many volunteer positions provide only basic accommodations, so don't expect room service or an ensuite bathroom.)

Volunteer Abroad (**www.volunteerabroad.com**) lists several organizations that provide volunteer opportunities for varying time periods. You'll need to check the individual websites, but many have no age limits. For example, one of the referenced websites is *Oyster* (**www.oysterworldwide.com**), which supports volunteer placements in several countries. Although some positions require experience, others only ask that you have an interest in the cause and be willing to work hard. The areas covered include animal welfare, conservation, and teaching, along with many others. With any program, consider how comfortable you'll be with the living conditions and the fact that you may be much older than most of the volunteers. But then, age is only a matter of attitude, right?

Mobility International (MIUSA) at **www.miusa.org** offers a variety of resources for people with disabilities to volunteer abroad with publications, travel tips, and inspirational stories of volunteers who did not let their physical challenges keep them from giving their time and energy to others.

Check the laws in the country where you want to volunteer to see what kinds of protections may be offered. While volunteer programs in the United States are required to provide reasonable accommodation for those with disabilities or other health conditions, those protections do not apply everywhere. You can find out more in MIUSA's publication, "Knowing Your Rights and Responsibilities" at **www.miusa.org/resource/tipsheet/rightsandresponsibilities**. Also see more information on traveling with a disability in the Appendix.

The best volunteers may be those with disabilities.

MIUSA features a short piece on its website, "The Dual Impact of Volunteering Abroad" by Megan Smith, who has volunteered in Costa Rica and Nepal. Smith points out that disabled volunteers are in a unique position, because they often need to ask for assistance or accommodations from the host community. That creates an interdependent relationship, where no one feels as if they are receiving charity. What better way to embrace our shared humanity than to share our strengths and look for assistance from each other when we need it?

Worldwide Opportunities on Organic Farms (WWOOF at www.wwoof.org).

If you're in good physical shape and have an interest in organic farming and alternative ways of living, then WWOOF may be your thing. Volunteers live on the host's farm and are provided with lodging and meals. You will work for about 4–6 hours a day, so you must be physically fit. You and your host negotiate the length of your stay. You are also responsible for obtaining any necessary visas. There is no age limit, and many hosts welcome mature WWOOFers. (If you have any physical limitations, you should disclose that to your host before completing your arrangements.) WWOOFing is also a good way to meet interesting people. There is a small charge to join.

Explore the benefits of house-swapping.

Kevin and I have friends who have house-swapped several times and have found it an affordable and pleasant way to vacation. While many people initially have fears about leaving their home open to strangers from another country for fear of theft or damage, house-swapping sites report that is almost never a problem. Instead, the biggest issue for house-swappers is that people have different cleaning standards. (Usually, that simply involves doing a little extra cleaning on arrival, or perhaps when you come home.) Remember, you'll be staying in your guests' house as well, and they may also have reservations about you!

Sometimes house-swappers make their vehicles available as well. If so, you need to check to see if your insurance will cover foreign visitors, and communicate with your counterpart to find out what's required for you to have insurance coverage on their vehicles.

Pets are another area of concern. If you're not comfortable leaving Fido and Fluffy with strangers, you will, of course, need to make other arrangements. And if you're expected to petsit as well as housesit, you need to know that in advance.

Most websites that organize house swaps require an annual fee of about $100 or so. However, many will give you an extra year if you don't find an exchange in the first 12 months. With all home exchanges, your best chance of a successful experience is to communicate extensively with the people you're exchanging with well before the swap. Also, if you're a perfectionist or are wary of cultural differences, then home-swapping may not be for you.

Here are some popular house-swapping sites. The first two have been used by friends:

HomeExchange.com (***www.homexchange.com***) claims to have more than 65,000 listings in more than 150 countries and offers a 14-day free trial. The site has facilitated more than a million exchanges since 1992.

Intervac (***www.intervac-homeexchange.com***), in business since 1953, bills itself as the "original home exchange service." The name comes from "international" and "vacation." The organization has more than 30,000 members and features a 20-day free trial.

Another popular site is *Homelink.com* (***www.homelink.com***), which also says it has been in business since 1953. To make things easier for first-timers, Homelink suggests a hospitality exchange, where members host each other while they are in their homes. They also advertise 27 multi-lingual representatives around the world to assist you in your own language should you need help.

Read these tips to be a good house-swapper.

If you decide you'd like to house-swap, here's some advice from a veteran:

1. Lock valuables away in a cabinet, closet, or safe.

2. Ask a neighbor or friend to be a contact for how things work in your house, in case your guests have difficulties figuring out the operation of appliances, alarms, or services in your home. Provide appliance manuals too.

3. Leave a list of local attractions and where the best places are to eat or buy groceries, along with other helpful items, such as where to get public transportation or which hours roads are likely to be crowded.

4. Although not required, it's nice if you can set up a social engagement, such as a coffee, with a neighbor or family member to help them get acquainted with the area.

If you're an academic, or a writer or an artist, *Sabbatical Homes* (*www.sabbaticalhomes.com*) may be right for you, although I do not know anyone who has used the site, so I would welcome some feedback. While its primary focus is on exchanges, the site also offers a few rentals along with house-sitting and sharing opportunities.

The grass is greener (and taller)!

Our friends, Americans who have participated in several exchanges, had an experience that shows why the best home-swappers are those who approach their house swap with the understanding that not everything may go as planned:

Returning home after their house swap with an Amsterdam couple, our friends found the grass on their lawn had sprouted several inches. They even had trouble cutting it with their lawnmower. Puzzled, because their Dutch guests had agreed to mow the lawn, our friends asked as tactfully as they could why the grass remained uncut. Finally, the Dutch couple sheepishly confessed: As lifelong dwellers in that city of canals, they had never mown a lawn before. Confronted with the unfamiliar machine, the visitors were simply too afraid to use it!

Find a house-sitting/pet-sitting gig.

Joining a house-sitting organization is another way to live abroad temporarily on a tight budget. The caveat is to know exactly what's expected, before you commit. Make sure you know the location, how accessible it is to the places you want to see, and how much of a time commitment you'll have to make. It's one thing to take care of a goldfish and another to manage an entire farm. We have not yet tried house-sitting, but it's on our list. However, while perusing the listings on some sites, I've realized that a few people just want slave labor. I don't know about you, but I don't want to live on a manor-house estate, if it means shoveling out stables and doing the gardening, so read carefully. Here are some of the most popular house-sitting websites:

Housecarers.com (**www.housecarers.com**), based in Australia, has been matching house-sitters and homeowners for more than 15 years. They have listings worldwide. As of 2016, the cost for a house-sitter to join the organization and set up a profile is $50. Travelers pay their own travel expenses. While rent is free, the house-sitter may be asked to pay for some utilities; those arrangements are negotiated with the sitter and homeowner.

TrustedHousesitters.com (**www.trustedhousesitters.com**) asks $8.25/month or $99/year. While they offer house-sitting assignments throughout the world, they appear to have an especially strong presence in Europe. A nice feature of the site is that it allows you to search not just by location but also by the type of house-sit (cat sits, dog sits, and summer-home sits, for example). TrustedHousesitters, like many other sites, also offers the opportunity for a daily email alert advising of new listings.

An online search will reveal other house-sitting organizations. As with any lodging, be suspicious if someone asks you to wire money. Reputable websites do not work that way.

Look for good-value budget accommodations.

While the following options are not free, they are relatively inexpensive and offer good value:

Stay at a college.

Many colleges and universities offer low-cost B&B accommodation for tourists during the summer season. Our two-night stay at *Keble College* in Oxford was a highlight of one trip to England, where we eagerly consumed an included full English breakfast in a grand, 300-seat medieval-appearing dining hall (though it was built in the 1870s). Its soaring ceiling and paneled walls transported us to another place, and while there were no owls or floating candles, we half-expected to see Harry Potter and his friends at the next table. The accommodation in a student room featured a queen-sized bed (two singles joined together) and a private bath. Though not luxurious, and a little on the small side, it was certainly clean and comfortable, with free linens, towels, and toiletries. And the opportunity to walk around the college and feel as though we were a part of Oxford was priceless.

Want to stay in a castle? *Durham Castle*, part of Durham University, also offers bed-and-breakfast at a reasonable price, and the atmosphere is hard to beat.

You can book accommodations for many colleges in Europe, Asia, and North America at *University Rooms* (**www.university-rooms.com**). Just be aware of the cancellation fees and know that if you must make changes, you need to contact University Rooms and not the colleges themselves.

Enjoy the peace of religious accommodations.

One of my fondest memories of our first trip to Europe was awakening in Rome to the sound of angels singing. Well, maybe they weren't angels, but the room we rented in a convent was right next door to the nuns' chapel. When I awoke, in my drowsy state, I half-believed the inspirational singing I heard was emanating from a heavenly throng. What a lovely way to wake up!

A quick web search, or a visit to your local library, will reveal several lodging guides for staying at convents, monasteries, and other religious accommodation, mostly in Europe. The website *Monastery Stays* (**www.monasterystays.com**) is an easy option for North American visitors since you won't have to struggle with language issues. Convents and monasteries offer a unique cultural stay, but they may not always offer the best prices. They typically have a curfew as well. You don't need to be Catholic or even religious. As religious guest houses, however, they ask you to act respectfully. In other parts of the world, you can also sometimes stay at Buddhist monasteries or other religious lodgings.

Rent a house or apartment.

My favorite house/cottage/apartment rental site is *Airbnb* (**www.airbnb.com**), which offers rentals around the world. The accommodations range from shared housing and private rooms to entire houses or apartments. Kevin and I prefer privacy, so we typically make sure to check "entire home" in the filters for housing choices (entire home, private room, shared room), although we sometimes rent a room with a private bathroom for short stays.

The best places are those that are run by friendly people who have a mother-in-law apartment or a vacation rental and who really try to ensure you have a wonderful time. Many hosts leave candies, a bottle of wine, or local specialties such as cheeses or drinks unique to their area. Lately, there have been many more offerings that are obviously run by commercial establishments that are listing more than one place. They may be perfectly adequate, but we much prefer the family-run places. In addition, both local governments and Airbnb are cracking down on hosts that are offering multiple listings, because they are contributing to a shortage in affordable housing.

One Airbnb practice that I really appreciate is that although they charge your credit card immediately, they do not release the funds to your hosts until you have been there 24 hours. (Full disclosure: We have always been reasonably happy with our Airbnb accommodation, so we have never had to call the number provided should you need help, but friends and relatives who have had issues have commented on Airbnb's exceptional customer service in resolving their problems.) I also like Airbnb's strong anti-discrimination policy.

We rented 25Airbnb lodgings on our RTW trip without experiencing any difficulties. Most places were better than advertised. A couple didn't quite measure up to their advertising, but in those cases I had not read deeply enough into the reviews. In any case, they were sufficient. Generally, if you read the reviews carefully, you'll know what you're getting. I try to select places that have multiple reviews and "read between the lines."

What does that mean? Here's an example: If a guest writes "I loved the central location, but there were a lot of revelers. We don't mind because we are sound sleepers," you definitely have a clue that it is noisy. I like knowing what to expect, but my pet peeve about reviews of budget lodging are those written by people who complain about something minor, as though they expect five-star accommodations when they are paying rock-bottom prices. Airbnb has higher-priced accommodations too, if you want to splurge.

Both Airbnb hosts and guests can review each other, so there is sometimes a tendency to hold back on criticism, which is why reading reviews carefully is important. But because Airbnb establishments are not hotels, and many are run by people who are simply trying to supplement their income, I don't think it's fair to slam your hosts if their coffeepot isn't up to your standards. If the bed is uncomfortable or the place isn't clean, that's another matter.

Airbnb isn't for everyone. If you're a perfectionist who has to have linens of a specific type, or if you're a cook who can't live without the right cooking pots, or if you absolutely must have superb lighting in your bathroom, then Airbnb may not be for you. However, many potential issues can be bypassed by reading the reviews in depth.

You meet the most interesting people through Airbnb.

Many of our richest travel experiences have come from our Airbnb hosts. We've met writers, artists, and other accomplished people who shared their hearts, talents, and minds with us. For example, in Florence, Italy, we stayed in a huge studio, decorated with the work of the host's artist father, and a view of the Duomo (cathedral) from our window that appeared so close we could almost touch it. Had his father not been ill, our host would have taken us to his family's country house, and he insisted we return so he could treat us. In Ireland, we rambled through a remote valley with only the wind and sheep for company, near the farm of the couple who hosted us, a talented potter and an accomplished artist. In Sydney, we learned about indigenous Australian art from our hosts, who knew some of the most famous artists. In other locations, our hosts went out of their way to take us to their special places. We also encountered Patrick, a New Zealander with a six-foot rabbit friend named Fred, a pookah like the one in "Harvey," the classic Jimmy Stewart film. We might have worried about our host because his giant rabbit, like Harvey, is invisible to most people. But Patrick explained that once he started posting about Fred on the online dating sites, the women who replied to him were much more creative, and he didn't want to meet women with no imagination! Patrick didn't miss a beat when I said, "I think I saw Fred the other day. Does he have a black-tipped ear?" "No," he replied. "But the tip of one was bitten off in a fight, so maybe that's what you saw." I've never had a conversation like that at a Marriott.

Other home rental sites that we have used include *VRBO* (**www. vrbo.com**) and *Homeaway* (**www.homeaway.com)**, where owners pay to list their places. I have noticed that some rates have creeped up on these sites in recent years, but you can often find bargains, especially if you're sharing accommodation with another couple or two. Other websites that I have not tried, but have been recommended to me, include *Wimdu* (**www.wimdu.com,** good for European rentals), *PandaBed* (**www.pandabed.com**, specializing in Asian rentals), and *FlipKey* (**www.flipkey.com**), which is owned by the TripAdvisor Media Group. *TripAdvisor* (**www.tripadvisor.com**) also lets you rent through its review site now. (See the Appendix for more recommendations on rentals in Europe.)

Wiring money, a favorite of con artists, is almost always a bad idea.

Although all the websites listed in this book are legitimate, you should know that sometimes unscrupulous people can take advantage of these services. Phishing — or publishing a website that looks very much like the original — is just one of the scams that can be used. If you book through a service such as Airbnb, make sure you *always* use the booking on the site itself. If someone sends you an email and says you can book with them directly, do not do it.

I broke my own rule once, but that was because I had extensively researched the couple who owned the cottage that we wanted to rent. A careful search revealed that they had another business in the area, and the family had lived on the property for more than 50 years. In addition, they were listed on the official town website, so I felt certain they were not a fly-by-night operation. In the rare instance that you need to wire money, *Xoom* (**www.xoom.com**), a PayPal company, is a reliable and inexpensive site for money transfers and is much cheaper than using a bank.

There are many other holiday rentals you can find throughout the world with a little searching. Although there are lodging listings online that are available through Craigslist and Gumtree (in the UK), I prefer to use established listing services for added security.

Use a real estate agent for long-term bookings.

It may not be easy to find them, but if you plan to stay in one location for months, consider renting through a real estate agent or rental broker, which can be cheaper. (However, some Airbnb listings also offer discounts for longer stays.) In the UK, *Rightmove* (**www.rightmove.co.uk**) lists both property for sale and for rent from local estate agents (realtors), and sometimes, particularly if you want to rent in winter, you can find great deals. (Make sure to check the appropriate filters and look for the rare listing that includes utilities and council taxes. Note that some of the cheaper prices are for house-sharing not for an entire place of your own.) Because it's difficult to identify a reputable agency online, you may wish to rent a place through Airbnb for a week or so and wait till you are in the locality to find an agent. Of course, that approach works better off-season.

Book hotels, hostels, and B&Bs with online sites.

We typically rely on conventional hotels and B&Bs only when we will be somewhere for one or two nights and our arrival or departure time is outside of normal business hours. Then I look for places with 24-hour reception desks. My favorite booking engines are *AARP Expedia* (**www.expedia-aarp.com**) and *Booking.com* (**www.booking.com**.) The latter also offers home/apartment and bed-and-breakfast bookings. (The AARP Expedia site states you will get the best price on hotels, whether that is through Expedia or your 10 percent AARP discount. Members also get a 25 percent savings and a one-car-group upgrade from Avis and Budget.)

I rely on AARP Expedia and Booking.com simply because I have found that those sites most often deliver what I want, and I don't always have time to do multiple searches. However, because situations change, it's a good idea to periodically check a service that compares multiple booking sites, such as *Kayak* (**www.kayak.com**) or *Trivago* (**www.trivago.com**) to see where you consistently get the best deals. Then, always do one last check on the hotel website to see if you can get an even better rate. In the Asia-Pacific region — Australia, Singapore, and Hong Kong — I have also found good deals on *Zuji* (**www.zuji.com**).

Some seniors like *Bed-and-Breakfast.com* (**www.bedandbreakfast.com**), but I find most of their listings to be in the splurge category.

You can also use *Priceline* (**www.priceline.com**) or *Hotwire* (**www.hotwire.com**) to bid on a hotel room, but then you must accept if the hotel agrees to your price.

Another tip: You may want to go to your control panel or settings to delete your web history before returning to booking sites. In the past, some web pages generated cookies, a means to track your device, and when you returned, the web pages would not always display the lowest priced option. While I'm not sure that's still a widespread phenomenon, it doesn't hurt to be sure. (You can always test it out. If you return to a site and can't find the fantastic deal you saw yesterday, delete your web history and see if that helps.)

Hostels may be an option.

There is no age limit at many hostels, and they can offer special value to the single traveler. (For more than two people, my experience is that you can often get a better deal through Airbnb.) My friends who use hostels swear by *Hostelworld* (**www.hostelworld.com**), which also lists some budget hotels and B&Bs. These days many hostels offer accommodation in private rooms as well as dorms, and some include ensuite bathrooms.

When you want to splurge, check out these sites!

If you want to rent an entire manor house or castle, take a look at *Scotts Castle Holidays* (***www.scottscastles.com***). Advertising more than 100 self-catering castles or large houses in England and Scotland, Scotts offers unique lodgings that can actually be fairly reasonable if you're sharing expenses with other couples. Along with some friends and family, Kevin and I rented a castle from Scotts several years ago and found it absolutely delightful! We had an entire estate to roam, the ruins of an old castle to explore, and a catered dinner of Scottish specialties to savor. We were entertained by a bagpiper, which Scotts helped arrange. We felt like real lairds and ladies, and by splitting the costs, our pocketbook was not hit hard.

I have also been intrigued with the cottage offerings of the *National Trust Holidays* (***www.nationaltrustholidays.org.uk/***), featuring unusual and historic lodgings that are often a part of large estates that are managed by the National Trust. Though a little higher priced, they appear to be furnished to a high standard. I haven't rented with them yet, but hope to one day.

Similarly, *The Landmark Trust* (***www.landmarktrust.org.uk/***) offers properties of character in Belgium, France, Italy, Scotland, Wales, Lundy, and the Channel Islands, in addition to mainland England. They offer multiple search criteria, including "gardens of beauty," "historic city breaks," "walking opportunities," "inspiring interiors," and "links to literature." The latter includes a rental of Casa Guidi in Florence, Italy, the former home of Robert and Elizabeth Barrett Browning. The Landmark Trust also offers bookings in a restored apartment in Rome, which overlooks the Piazza di Spagna, that is identical to one, a floor below, where John Keats lived. (Again, if you share, the per-person rates can be reasonable.)

Explore additional resources.

Check the official tourist websites for the countries you wish to visit, because they will often have listings of local places to rent. Years ago, we rented a cottage in Oia, on the Greek Island of Santorini, that was built right into the cliff. At the time, a government program sponsored artists and villagers to revive the village for tourism. They succeeded. Our cottage was very cheap (less than $20 a night), but today, Oia is tourist hotspot and one-bedroom cottages like ours now rent for nearly $200 a night. What you want to do is find the next hotspot, before it becomes one. Let me know what you find at *www.seniorbudgettravel.com*.

See this checklist before you book.

When you are arranging your accommodations, here's a list of the things you want to ask about or check first:

☐ Do you know where the room/apartment/house is located and how to get there? Sometimes online sites group rentals in a particular location with towns nearby (or not so nearby), so you need to be sure you know the exact position. Many sites include maps, which are helpful.

☐ If you need to depend on public transportation, how much will it cost to get to the location from your previous destination and how often does the bus or train run? In rural locations, services may run only a few times a week. However, if you can stay outside the center of a main city and get to the main tourist sites within minutes, then you can frequently save a lot of money. Also see if the local public transportation offers discounts for seniors.

☐ If you're renting a car, is there free parking? If not, how much can you expect to pay at nearby parking lots ("car parks")? We once rented an apartment in Dubrovnik thinking that free parking was nearby, based on a review. But the free parking was no longer available. It was only because our host was particularly helpful that we managed to secure a parking place at no charge. Without her assistance, we would have burst our budget, paying close to $20 per night more.

☐ What is the general layout? Some rentals require you to access one bedroom by going through another. That might not be a problem with a family, but if you're traveling with two couples that could be a deal-breaker. Be sure to ask whether the bedrooms have separate access if you have any doubts.

☐ How accessible is the place you're renting? If the listing says "a few steps" find out what it means. Access from the street to an apartment, or even access from an elevator, may not be direct. (If you're like me ten steps might be doable, but forty would be a problem.) Also, be aware that in Europe, what we call the "first floor" in the US is the "ground floor," so if an apartment is listed on the "second floor," it would be on the "third floor" in the United States. That might mean you'll have to climb more stairs than you planned.

☐ Does the rental have the amenities you need? For example, it is common in many parts of the world to have a washer but not a gas or electric clothes dryer. If you feel you must have a dryer, not a drying rack — although that system works well — you may have to visit the local laundromat. If so, do you know how far the local laundromat or "launderette" is?

In any case, be prepared for the energy-saving washers and dryers to be smaller and take much longer to complete their cycles than those in the US or Canada.

How I became "the angel of the washing place."

It was one of the best titles I ever earned. Yet I achieved that designation only because laundromats operate in maddeningly different ways. Fortunately, there is usually someone to help. In one laundromat in Florence, Italy, I was the beneficiary of a woman who used charade-like gestures to show me how the washers worked. Later, two young women students from Croatia and Brazil entered, and I passed along the favor. They put their clothes in the machine and took off. When they returned, several minutes later, I was in the process of showing a young man how to navigate the system. "Oh how nice," the Croatian student said to me, "you are truly the angel of the washing place!"

Can you decode the symbols on foreign appliances?

Ovens are not common in many places in the world. Even rentals that have a stovetop may not necessarily have an oven. If that's important to you, be sure to ask before booking.

Having a cooktop or oven not only saves you money, it also gives you the opportunity to cook wonderful local foods. You can make memorable meals with fresh produce and specialties, like cheese and

wine, from open-air markets and from the aromatic breads and tan-
talizing pastries from the local bakeries.

However, you may find the symbols on your appliances confus-
ing. (I remember once in Croatia, I could not figure out how to turn
the oven on. I asked Kevin to help, and he was able to do so, but he
couldn't explain how he had done it.) If you have trouble decipher-
ing the symbols, do a web search using phrases like "European oven
symbols" or "Asian washing machine symbols," but realize you may
have to resort to trial and error.

Is the bed fit for a queen?

Another important category: beds. A queen or king bed in the
United States is not the same as a queen bed or king bed elsewhere.
In Europe and elsewhere, a queen is often two single beds joined
together, but the measurements are different. If you're very tall, be
very sure you're getting a bed that can accommodate your larger
frame.

For example, in the US and Canada, a queen bed measures 60
inches by 80 inches (152 centimeters by 203 centimeters). But a
European queen bed is 63 inches by 79 inches (160 centimeters by
200 centimeters). King beds are also slightly different. If bed size is
important to you, you can find a worldwide comparison by doing a
web search on "bed size" + "Wikipedia" for a handy reference sheet.

Find the right mix to save cash.

We try to choose lower cost accommodations that we feel comfortable with, and then splurge from time to time on nicer "digs" to
keep our budget in line and our spirits intact. Even relatively simple
accommodations can deliver something special such as a view or

balcony, or they can offer characteristic local charm to make your stay rewarding. Find the mix that works for you, and wherever you go, live life to the fullest!

CHAPTER 4:

PREPARING TO GO

With everything settled at home, you can relax in your own paradise.

N ow that you have figured out at least the first part of your itinerary, it's time to refine your plan and gear up to make it happen.

Revise your itinerary.

Take out the calendar and itinerary you created previously. If you're on track, you have now done the following:

- ☐ Decided where you want to go.

- ☐ Researched transportation costs and chosen your modes of travel, using Rome2Rio or other sites.

- ☐ Chosen your accommodations for the first month or so.

- ☐ Now it's time to adjust your initial plan. Don't worry, you'll be continually revising as you go, but having the first part of your journey organized will stand you well as you proceed. After you have booked transportation to your first destination, start making your reservations for at least the first several weeks of your trip.

I recommend using the *TripIt* app (***www.tripit.com***) to keep track of your reservations and make it easy to access that critical information while you are on the go. Be sure to review your reservations carefully, however. Because some countries put the day before the month when listing a date (for example, June 3, 2017, would be 03/06/17 in Europe rather than 06/03/17), TripIt will occasionally place your reservation in the wrong order. (Although that has only happened to me once.)

Tackle the ins and outs of insurance for travel.

Preparing for travel also means deciding whether to purchase comprehensive travel insurance, travel medical (health) insurance, a medical evacuation policy, or to take a chance and go without any additional cover.

Travel insurance presents several issues for senior travelers, primarily because the older you are, the more expensive it is and the harder it is to get. Even for a journey of a few weeks, travel insurance can add substantially to your costs, and a multi-week or multi-month trip makes it even pricier. Let's take a look at the options.

What kind of insurance do you need?

Comprehensive travel insurance covers not only emergency medical charges but also such things as trip cancellation, lost luggage, trip delays, and medical evacuation, along with other losses that you may incur while traveling. Although you can sometimes buy individual coverages for specific items (for example, for trip cancellation), most people buy comprehensive travel insurance. If you want that coverage, however, you often need to buy it as soon as you have booked (or shortly thereafter) to qualify for reimbursement of your expenses. By contrast, travel health/medical insurance, which covers only emergency medical care (and sometimes repatriation of remains), normally only needs to be purchased before you leave for your trip.

What will Medicare cover?

If you're only going to be gone for 60 days, some Medicare policies will reimburse you for emergency medical care for the first 60 days outside of the country. (Check your own Medicare plan.) But for longer travels, 60 days is obviously not enough.

Deciding what type of insurance to buy, if any, is not an easy task and one that we can only answer for ourselves. Check out the information below before you decide:

- Do a web search on "World Nomads Travel Insurance" to reach the quote engine for this site. We found good comprehensive travel coverage through them at a reasonable price for our RTW trip. However, they will offer you coverage only if you are under the age of 70. If you are older, they will refer you to another company.

- See *BootsnAll* (*www.bootsnall.com/travel-insurance/travel-medical-insurance.html*) or do a web search for "BootsnAll + travel + insurance" for a handy guide to compare quotes from five plans, which offer a variety of options. Some even cover pre-existing conditions, with caveats, although you can expect to be hit with high deductibles of several thousand dollars. See the page for Expat Insurance if you will be gone from home for more than six months. (Click "Expat" near the bottom of the page under "Find Insurance For Your Travel Style.")

- Two other good sources for finding travel insurance are *InsureMyTrip* (*www.insuremytrip.com*) and *Squaremouth* (*www.squaremouth.com*). Read the reviews and the fine print for each offering, as you would for any insurance product.

You can sometimes save money by buying a travel medical policy that excludes coverage in the United States. If you are a US resident on Medicare, that may make sense, although you still take a risk if you're ill or injured abroad and are unable to travel home.

Allianz Global Assistance (*www.allianztravelinsurance.com*) offers several plans, including per trip or annual plans available to those over the age of 70.

WEA health plans (***www.weadirect.com***), a division of the PA Group — rated A by independent insurance company analyst A.M. Best — also provides long-term plans for expatriates and long-term travelers.

Consider evacuation services.

What do you do if you just feel that comprehensive travel and travel medical insurance are both too expensive or the coverage for your pre-existing condition is too high? You could decide to shorten your trip to obtain affordable coverage, particularly if you have a life-threatening condition. Or you could choose an evacuation service. Because medical costs in the United States are the highest in the world, many travelers plan to pay for minor ailments abroad out of their savings. If you do that, then you could sign up for a medical evacuation policy that will bring you home if you are seriously ill or injured and admitted to a hospital. (Note, however, that these services typically require admission to a hospital before you can be evacuated.) It's still somewhat risky, because you might not be stable enough to be moved. However, if you have enough savings, that's a chance you may want to take, given the extremely high costs of travel insurance for mature travelers.

Learn about evacuation policies available through Medjet Assist.

Medjet Assist (***www.medjetassist.com***) provides medical transport to the hospital of your choice if you are injured or become ill abroad — as long as you are admitted to a hospital first. It's important to note that Medjet Assist takes you to the hospital of *your choice*, because some other evacuation policies will only take you to the nearest hospital that the company deems adequate. With Medjet

Assist, your annual membership is all you'll pay. The service will also cover you in the United States when you are more than 150 miles from home. If you are a member of AARP, you can get discounts; for example, an individual membership that is normally $270 will cost $235 and a family membership, which is normally $395, costs $345 for members up to the age of 75. Medjet Assist also covers repatriation of remains.

Decide how you want to handle things back home.

For peace of mind, you'll want to make sure that you've completed your arrangements at home before you leave. Will you leave your residence vacant, asking a friend or family member to check up on it from time to time? Will you move out of rental accommodation and put your worldly goods in storage? Or will you lease or sublet?

Should you rent or sublet?

If you're away only for a few weeks or if you're involved in a home exchange, you won't need to worry about renting or subleasing your home. But if you decide to rent or sublease, you'll need to check with your landlord. Do you own a condo? You'll need to review your association's rules and covenants, including any time requirements or rules about pets. (For example, our own condo association only allows rentals of more than six months, does not accept dogs, and charges a hefty nonrefundable fee for the privilege of renting, in addition to deposits, which we had to add to our budget.)

If you rent or sublease, you'll also want to have a property manager or someone who can be contacted in case of an emergency at your rental. If you're lucky, a responsible family member or friend will play that role, especially because paying the fees of a professional property manager might add considerably to your expenses.

You will need to set up a separate account for your rental, for ease of use and for tax purposes. The IRS does not want you to co-mingle your personal and business funds, and even though you're renting your own residence, your rental will be considered a business. (Ask your accountant.) It's a good idea to keep a deposit in the rental account at all times to cover emergencies such as appliance repairs. Many municipalities also have strict requirements for landlords that typically favor the tenant, so you'll want to research your legal rights and responsibilities. (For example, in our area, there are limits on how soon landlords must respond to emergencies, as well as the procedures they, or their property managers, must follow to respect tenant privacy and rights.)

Finding a renter can seem like a daunting task, but it need not be. However, you want to be very careful about whom you trust with your home when you are far away. If you do not use a property manager's services and are renting yourself, check online with your local housing office to find out what you legally can and cannot do. (For example, where I live, you can't advertise for a "mature" renter, because that could be construed as age discrimination. And, indeed, we could care less about the age of the tenant; we simply didn't want partiers! So when I advertised our condo, I described the condo complex as one that was "very quiet and had a high percentage of residents who were over 55," which was all true and helped us to attract the type of renter we wanted.)

If you're not using a realtor as a property manager, who can advise you on all aspects of renting, how do you find out what to charge? Start with the local listings. You can see what similar places in your area are renting for. Just be completely honest with yourself:

Is your property truly comparable? Does it have all the amenities described in the listings you're using as a reference? Are your appliances, kitchens, and baths as up-to-date as the ones in the listings? It's helpful to visit those rentals, if you can, and put yourself in the mind of a prospective tenant.

Craigslist, Zillow, and other online sites allow you to place free advertisements for renters. However, always — *always* — check your prospective tenants carefully. You can download standard legal rental agreements for your state online, which should include a notice to the prospective tenant that, by signing, they are authorizing a credit check. Ask for references as well — and call them personally.

It is worth using a reliable service, such as *Experian* or *TransUnion SmartMove,* to do a credit check. There will typically be a charge, which some landlords pass on to the prospective tenant. Some services actually require prospects to order their own report and make it available to you. If you have friends who rent properties, you can also ask for their suggestions on which credit-checking services they use. *Whatever you do, do not skip this very important step and be sure to ask for references.*

Requiring a damage deposit and asking for the first and last months' rent helps with tenant-screening too, because those with financial difficulties may well have problems coming up with required funds — which can be a red flag. If you're going to be gone for months, you want a tenant who is reliable and pays on time.

What's more, if you rent out your home, be sure to get insurance on the residence itself, just in case something happens while you're gone. Your tenants can get renters insurance for their goods, and insuring your premises will be inexpensive compared to a homeowner's policy.

Consider utilities, whether you rent or not.

Most of the time renters are responsible for all utilities, but there are situations when you may want to pay a utility and simply increase the rent to cover it. You can then advertise it as a benefit. For example, some landlords prefer to cover items such as trash collection and landscaping to keep their properties looking attractive. Also, some utilities will charge an owner if a tenant fails to pay a bill. So take time to think about which, if any, bills you want to pay and make sure those utility payments are clearly stipulated in your rental agreement.

If you're going away for only a few months and you can afford to leave your place vacant, ask your utility companies if they have a vacation plan. Cable and telephone companies will often let you pay a substantially reduced rate while you're away, which means you can avoid the hassles and expenses of reconnecting when you return.

If you plan to be gone for a year or more and want to keep your phone number, it's also worth asking your landline provider if you can pay a small fee to retain the number. (See below "Using phone abroad? Choose the solution that works best for you.")

What are you going to do with your pet?

It probably goes without saying that the furry, feathered, or finned members of your family need to be considered when you plan your trip. The best arrangement for them is staying with family or friends who adore them. If you do a home exchange or are advertising for a housesitter, find out if your exchange partners or housesitters will be comfortable caring for your pets.

If those options don't work, check with your vet, who may have some contacts for pet care. In any case, make sure they are well provided for, or postpone your trip. (Editorial: Animals are not disposable! They have their own needs and emotions. I have no respect for anyone who would surrender their pets just to travel, but if you believe that is your only choice, then find them a good home or place them in a no-kill shelter and contribute funds to their care. You owe it to them!)

Get tips on storing your vehicle.

Are you planning to store a vehicle for the duration of your long-term trip? *Edmunds* (**www.edmunds.com**) has some advice on "How to Prep Your Car for Long-term Storage" on its website. Among the tips:

- Keep your car in a garage, if possible. If it will be outdoors, get a weatherproof car cover.

- Clean your vehicle before storing it. Bird droppings or water stains can damage the paint over time.

- Change the oil if you are storing the vehicle longer than 30 days.

- Top off the tank to keep moisture from forming inside the fuel tank, and keep seals from drying out.

- Make sure that the battery stays charged. Have someone start the car and drive it for at least 15 minutes every two weeks. Run the air conditioner too. If you can't get someone to drive it, then either disconnect the negative battery cable or use a trickle charger. (If you disconnect the battery charger, you'll lose the electronic settings for your radio, clock, and other settings.)

- Don't use the parking brake — use a chock to keep your vehicle in place.

- Check to see if your tires are properly inflated.

- Try to cover gaps where mice or other creatures can enter. Also try scent deterrents.

- Maintain your auto insurance. You may need only to keep the comprehensive insurance if no one is going to be driving it, but it will help protect you from damages that could result from problems at the storage location.

If someone is going to be driving your vehicle, make sure that you not only have the right insurance, but that you also keep the license tabs current. Most localities now allow you to pay your license fees online.

Find the right place to store furniture and personal items.

Unless you are going to rent your home furnished, you will need to store your furniture. In any case, you'll want to have a place to keep your personal items. If you have a family member or friend with extra space, they might just become your favorite person, because storage can be expensive.

Before our RTW trip we chose a storage facility that was close to our son's house, because he acted as our property manager. What made that choice even better was that his house was farther from an urban area, so the prices were lower there too. We chose a controlled atmosphere storage facility, which helps prevent problems due to heat, cold, or humidity.

Before you store anything, use your trip as an opportunity to get rid of the items that you "might need some day." It can be liberating to get rid of the "junk" that seems to multiply in our closets. Here are some tips:

- Take photos of the items that you treasure for sentimental reasons but you never use, and then donate them. You'll have the photos to recall those special memories.

- Give some of your best things to your friends, or ask them to keep treasures like Aunt Hattie's silver fruit bowl until you return.

- Put small items such as watches and jewelry in a safe deposit box at your bank.

- Take advantage of charity shops. Give away your serviceable items, and get a receipt for a tax deduction. Do good for others as you free yourself for your adventure.

- Host a garage sale or use Craigslist to sell items and get some extra cash.

- Consider consignment furniture stores, but make sure you know how long they will keep your items for sale and what they do with items that do not sell.

Also, if you have a relative whose place is serving as your temporary address, you may be able to get a policy from your own insurance company to cover your goods in storage. That policy may be cheaper than the insurance offered by the storage company.

Manage your banking online.

Many seniors are nervous about online banking. I understand that feeling, but I still strongly recommend banking over the Internet. Otherwise, you are stuck having a relative or friend back home manage your banking for you.

Yes, there is always some security risk, just as there is with banking in person, relying on a friend or family member ("Oh, sorry, I forgot to make that deposit!"), or with anything in life. After all, financial institutions are required by law to have multiple levels of security online, and there are things you can do to help ensure that your Internet-based transactions are safer:

- I strongly recommend using a VPN (virtual private network) whenever you are online and do not control access to the network. Public Wi-Fi and other Internet connections are often insecure, and unscrupulous people can use software to capture your passwords and data. I have personally used *SurfEasy* (***www.surfeasy.com***), a free VPN, and I am very happy with it. In addition, publications like *CNET* (***www.cnet.com***) and *PC Magazine* (***www.pcmag.com***) periodically rate security software, both free and paid, so those websites are good resources.

- Never save the passwords for your financial institutions in your browser, and always use a different username and password for each bank.

- Double-check that you entered the correct web address (URL) for the bank.

- When you log into your account, check to see that the address is prefaced by https (For example: ***https://www.***

[bankname].com/). The "s" indicates a secure site. You can also look for a padlock or key icon in the search box at the top of the web page. Those icons show that your transactions are being encrypted, giving you more peace of mind.

- Monitor your accounts frequently while you are traveling. (We had our credit card data stolen twice on our round-the-world trip, but we caught both instances early, notified our banks, and lost no money. Interestingly, both breaches were from ATM machines. We discovered the hard way that it is best to use ATMs inside of banks whenever possible.)

In addition, check out the AARP primer, "Seniors Guide to Online Banking":

http://www.aarp.org/money/budgeting-saving/info-07-2013/seniors-guide-online-banking.html.

Online banking makes traveling so much easier! You can pay bills and transfer funds with ease. You can have your Social Security and pension checks deposited automatically and use your credit card to withdraw funds from ATMs when traveling. (We set up transfers between our checking account and our Charles Schwab account and used our bank card to get cash. See the sidebar below, "Charles Schwab charges no ATM or foreign-exchange fees.")

Using phones abroad? Choose the solution that works best for you.

Check out the options below before you take your smartphone or standard cellphone with you. Remember, you can use your phone without charge with a messaging or voice app on a free Wi-Fi connection. *However, if you do that, be sure to turn off roaming in your phone settings.* (Apple iPhone users can go to Settings>Mobile

Data>Data Roaming, and Android phone users can disable data roaming at Settings>Mobile Networks. You may also have to enable Wi-Fi calling if you want to use a voice app for phone calls.) If you fail to turn off data roaming, you may face thousands of dollars in unwanted charges. (That advice is also true for US travelers who go to Canada and Mexico, even though those countries may be "next door.") Here are some other choices for phone use abroad:

Get an international plan from your existing carrier.

You can purchase an international plan from your existing cell-phone provider. It's worth checking with your carrier to see if they offer international plans, because depending on how long you are traveling and where you are going, they could make sense for you. They don't work for me, because I find them too expensive for long-term travel. You'll want to make sure that your phone is unlocked (see sidebar "Is my cellphone unlocked?" below) and that it is a quad-band phone that uses the GSM standard (GSM 850/900/1800/1900), which is common internationally. Sprint and Verizon formerly used another standard but now also offer world phones that can work on GSM networks. If you buy a new phone, make sure it is unlocked.

I don't recommend international SIMs!

For our RTW trip, I initially bought international SIM cards online that were advertised to work almost anywhere—but they often didn't. (SIM cards are the tiny plastic inserts inside your phone that provide your carrier connection.) Then, when I used one to place a call back to the United States, I couldn't get it to work on the automated phone tree. When requested to "enter 1 for yes" and "enter 2 for no," the pushed digits failed to register. As a result, I don't recommend international SIMs.

Use a local SIM in each locale.

In Europe and Asia, SIM cards are much cheaper than they are in the US, and you can buy them in several locations, including phone stores, small groceries, and sometimes even at newspaper kiosks. They are surprisingly affordable. In Spain, I once bought a SIM that was good for a week but cost me only about $3! When combined with an IDphonecard.com number (see below), you can make both local and international calls very inexpensively. The downside is that SIMs may work only in one country or incur data-roaming charges outside of the country.

Is my cellphone unlocked? What if it's not?

If you aren't sure if your phone is unlocked, switch SIM cards with a friend who uses another carrier. (Of course, your phones need to take a SIM of the same size.) If your phone works, it's unlocked. If your phone is not unlocked, you can usually call your carrier and ask them to unlock it — with one big caveat — you must meet the carrier's requirements. For example, you must have paid off your contract or have met certain time, usage, or payment limits. To get your phone unlocked, you will need to have your account number, the IMEI number (a unique identifying number) of your device, your phone number, and depending on the carrier, possibly your Social Security number. (To find your IMEI, dial *#06#, and the number should display for GSM phones.)

Phone rentals can break the bank!

Although there are services, such as Cellular Abroad, that offer phone rentals, I am not covering them here because I think budget travelers can do better with other options. If you don't have a suitable phone to take with you, you can almost always buy cheap phones and get a local SIM chip.

I recommend IDphonecard.com (www.idphonecard.com).

Kevin and I have used *IDphonecard* for more than 10 years, and we love it! In many places, this is the best way to call home cheaply from abroad. Rates in Europe are especially low. After you load your account with your credit card, it is debited only as you use it. There are no minimum monthly charges, so if you don't use your phone, you aren't charged.

IDphonecard works from any phone — a landline, a pay phone, or a cellphone. We use it at home to make international calls too. When you sign up with IDphonecard.com, you are assigned a PIN. You simply call a local toll-free number (listed on their website), enter the PIN, and then enter the phone number you are calling. It's easy. Call rates vary by country.

Look into VoIP services that let you take your phone number with you.

If you plan to rent a house or apartment that has a modem, you can look into voice-over-IP (VoIP) devices, such as Ooma (***www. ooma.com***) and magicJack (***www.magicjack.com***), that let you take your local phone number with you and call free to the US and Canada using the Internet. You simply plug in the device. (Reportedly, you also get low international rates to other countries,) We know an

American expat couple in Mexico who use Ooma and, after purchasing the device, they currently pay just a little over $5.00 per month for the service. Of course, that doesn't help with calls from your cellphone.

Explore Skype, FaceTime, and messaging apps.

If you're new to Skype or FaceTime, this might be the time to get to know them. These online services are a delight for grandparents, because, as long as you and your callers have a laptop or tablet with a front-facing camera, you can not only talk, you can also see that sweet, talented grandchild. The only drawback is that you need a strong Internet connection for best results, and in some parts of the world that's not a given. (However, I must say that we have found better Internet connections in some still-developing countries than on the Oregon and California coasts.)

You can also download messaging apps such as *WhatsApp* that will allow you to text family and friends through an Internet connection on your cellphone or computer, as long as both you and the contact have downloaded the app. Or, if you have an Apple phone, you can iMessage anyone with an iPhone or iPad to stay in touch.

Find the credit card that's right for you.

Several months before you leave, review your credit cards to determine whether the bank charges a fee for foreign transactions (in addition to the normal rate of currency exchange) or a fee for ATM withdrawals. You should be able to find this information on the financial institution's website, or you can call their customer service number.

Many banks have relationships with other banks around the world, which can help the traveler avoid ATM costs, so check that out too. (For example, Bank of America partners with Barclay's in the UK, PNB Paribas in France, Deutsche Bank in Germany, and China Construction Bank in mainland China, so there is no ATM fee for using your Bank of America Visa card at those banks' ATM machines.)

Avoid ATM and foreign exchange fees — and be prepared.

As noted previously, our Charles Schwab account is linked with our bank account, so when we travel we can easily transfer funds between them. Then we can use our Schwab card to obtain funds abroad, since Schwab does not charge a foreign transaction or ATM fee.

We typically take three different bank cards when we travel, which we split between the two of us. That way we have a backup. This practice was helpful when we had a credit card (not our Schwab card!) compromised.

Review your statements frequently as you travel and call your bank at once if you notice unexplained charges. If you need a new card mailed to you and don't have a secure address, look for name-brand mail services that you are familiar with. We found a Mail Boxes Etc. center in Italy that worked well as an address to have a replacement card sent to us.

Also, check the expiration dates on your credit cards before you leave, and if you discover they will expire before you return, call the bank's customer service number. Many banks will issue new cards for you with an expiration date that will take you beyond your time of travel. Just ask.

Set up your mail service weeks before you leave.

The US Postal Service will only hold your mail at the post office for up to 30 days, so long-term travelers will need to find another solution. Today, many companies will send you bills by email or by electronic billing to your bank, which simplifies bill paying enormously. You can also set up autopay for many accounts.

But what do you do about other correspondence? As with other items that must be managed when you're away, you can always rely on a neighbor, relative, or friend to retrieve your mail, sort it, and contact you about the important messages. The US Postal Service will only forward mail for a year. After that, it is returned to the sender. That's why it's important to notify all your creditors and correspondents of your new mailing address.

During our round-the-world trip we had some mail (correspondence from our accountant and tax information, for example) sent to our son's house. We planned to do our tax return by email and phone (which worked well by the way), so we wanted to be sure we wouldn't miss key documents. For all other mail, we used an online mail service.

For both our year-plus trip and our nearly three-month trip to Paris the year before, we relied on *Traveling Mailbox* (**www.traveling-mailbox.com**). We found them to be reliable and reasonably priced. The company's excellent customer service team also responded quickly whenever we had a question.

When you sign up with Traveling Mailbox, you get an actual street mailing address with a box number. The service scans your mail and posts it on a secure website online. Wherever you are, you can review the scanned envelope and direct them to either scan the contents, shred and delete the mail piece, or forward it for a small additional fee. Traveling Mailbox currently charges $15/month to scan 40 incoming envelopes and scan 35 pages of content; for $25/month, they will scan 100 envelopes and scan 80 interior pages.

My only caveat is to make sure you know exactly how to complete the USPS form that allows them to accept your mail, because the instructions were slightly difficult to understand. Again, the customer service at Traveling Mailbox is quite helpful if you have problems.

Whether you use a mail service or a local contact, be sure to make your arrangements several weeks before you leave to make sure everything is working smoothly. Equally important, when you return home, be sure to notify all your correspondents of your change of address and make sure the mail is being delivered to your "new" (old) home address before stopping your mail-service arrangements. If you have any problems, the USPS toll-free number (1-800-275-8777) is very helpful.

Prepare for your health needs.

Of course, you'll want to be sure you are healthy before you travel. It's a good idea to have a thorough check-up a few months before you leave and plan to visit a travel clinic. For more information see, chapter 5, "Staying Healthy While Traveling."

Follow these tips to make your trip safer.

In most parts of the world, the biggest threat you face is not to your personal safety, but to the loss of your personal items. For the most part, use common sense and take a few precautions:

- As at home, be aware of your surroundings. Walk in well-lighted areas and in places where there are other people.

- Learn the obvious cons — people who have found a ring and want to sell it to you, young people with clipboards who say they are collecting for charity, and anyone that wants to "give" you something or have you write a postcard to their nephew in America. If someone on the street asks you if you speak English, be wary. It's sometimes a set-up. And be alert to anyone who tries to distract you with a spill on your jacket or some commotion, a favorite trick of pickpockets.

- Leave your expensive jewelry at home. No need to tempt thieves, and besides, it is easy to lose small items, so why chance that? It's also culturally sensitive to avoid appearing too flashy in developing countries where a single piece of your jewelry may be worth more than most people earn in a year.

- Minimize hassles by planning. Use money belts or special clothing (T-shirts, socks, etc.) that conceal cash and credit cards. Many are protected from electronic theft, so that thieves can't invisibly "read" your credit cards with special devices as they pass by.

- Keep your purse close to your body and away from the street, where someone on a scooter could snatch it. Keep only a small amount of cash in your wallet and don't keep it in a back or outside pocket.

- Leave your smartphone in your bag when you're not using it. Don't sit it down on a counter or table when you stop to have a coffee or lunch, or you could be bidding it goodbye.

Remember, should you have a serious emergency, such as a lost passport, contact the US Consulate. (But theft needs to be reported to the local police first.) If you're a victim of theft, don't be too embarrassed to admit it, and don't let it ruin your trip!

If you're away during an election, find out how you can vote.

It's easy to vote while you're away. The law requires that all US citizens abroad be allowed to receive their ballots and vote electronically. Depending on your state, you can get your ballot by email, fax, or Internet download. Get all the information you need on voting absentee by checking with your county elections office, or go to *www.FVAP.gov* and complete an application, which you can send to your local elections office.

Pack light for your adventure.

At last, the time is growing short, and it's time to pack. I'll make you a bet: You will never find any book on budget travel that does not tell you to pack light! There's a reason for that. Not only is a lot of luggage cumbersome, but even if you plan to use taxis, they're a big hit on your budget, and they're not always easy to find. Particularly if you're senior, you do not want to be putting strain on aging vertebra and muscles by wrestling with heavy luggage.

I'm not going to provide an extensive list on what to pack. You can find suggestions in multiple guidebooks, and you can see packing tips online. YouTube (*www.youtube.com*) for example, will show you videos on how to pack light. What I will do is share a few packing tips and tricks that I have found most helpful.

What luggage works best?

Whether we travel for a few weeks or for months on end, Kevin and I travel with the same bags: a carry-on size piece of rolling luggage and a small day-pack each. The carry-ons may sometimes be zipped out to their fullest (so they no longer qualify as carry-ons on many airlines), but they are still lightweight, and in a pinch, we can carry them. We prefer not to use hard-sided luggage because we can get more into soft-sided bags, but that's purely your choice.

If you purchase rolling bags, make sure the rollers on them are not the free-spinning kind that move in all directions. While touted as an advantage, wheels that move every which way can be hard to control on the cobblestone paving and rough streets in much of the world.

Day packs are handy for carrying extra clothing, umbrellas, and when you get settled, you can use them for a packed picnic lunch. I also put toiletries in mine, and leave the toiletries at the apartment or hotel when I am out and about.

Speaking of toiletries, unless you are really "married" to a particular product (and sometimes that makes sense for your hair or skin type), don't stress over packing enough. You can find many of your favorite brands worldwide, and if you have to use another, you may discover a new favorite.

Use packing bags or cubes to pack more items.

Many people favor packing cubes for putting their clothing inside of their suitcase. I prefer vacuum bags — the kind that have a closing like a zip-lock bag and require you to push the air out by rolling them up from the bottom. I can get up to one-third more items in my suitcase that way.

Do my clothes wrinkle? A little, but not that much. I try to choose fabrics such as knits that resist wrinkling. I also pack a small empty spray bottle. I fill the bottle with water and spray my clothing before I take a shower, taking time to smooth out the fabric with my hand. I hang the items that I intend to wear later in the bathroom, and while I am showering the steam completes the job. I don't find it worthwhile to bring a travel iron. If you are attending an event where every crease must be pressed, most hotels and apartments will have an iron that you can borrow.

Pack clothing that you will wear.

Many guides list specific items that you should take with you. But it really depends on you. For example, I have often read suggestions to pack sandals or flip-flops with you when going to a beach. But I don't like wearing sandals or flip-flops! I prefer to wear slip-on shoes, so obviously, I am not going to take sandals just because some guidebook says I should.

Some guides tell you not to pack jeans, because they can take a long time to dry when laundered. But if you live in jeans at home, you won't want to be without them. In most of the world today, people wear jeans, which wasn't true 20 years ago. Yes, there are places, like the opera, where you shouldn't wear them, but for basic sight-seeing, comfort counts.

The best advice for travel clothing, unless you know you will be perpetually in summer or in winter, is to pack in layers. Take tops and sweaters, and you will be set for all but the coldest weather when you can take a coat with you.

For women, packing with a basic color scheme that allows the mixing and matching of tops and bottoms (slacks or skirts) works well. I also like to include one nice dress, along with flats that I can wear to the theater or dressier places, and they do double duty as slippers. (Anything that has more than one purpose is the way to go! I have even used a pajama top as an extra top for jeans—but don't tell anyone.) And scarves and accessories can really change an outfit.

My husband, Kevin, refuses to pack dress shoes, because they are heavy and he says it's not worth it for the few times he would wear them. So he packs nice walking shoes that can morph into business-casual dress. Or sometimes he packs lightweight leather loafers that can work for dressier occasions. We aim to be presentable, but we're not necessarily the most stylish, all in the name of avoiding hefty luggage.

If you find later that you really need a particular item of clothing and regret leaving it behind, that can actually be an advantage, because it gives you an excuse to buy an article that then becomes your souvenir. (And no, that isn't why I am continually losing my sweaters and jackets!)

What about special equipment?

Whether you should bring your own snorkel gear, hiking boots, walking sticks, or other equipment is up to you. Much depends on where you'll be spending most of your time. For example, if I were only going to be snorkeling for one week in a multi-month trip, I would not pack my own gear; I'd rent it. But if I were planning to spend months in the South Pacific, I would bring my own snorkel and mask. Remember in most resort locations, you can rent equipment, but it's usually expensive. You have to balance your needs, time, and the hassle of packing your special items.

Another example: We do a lot of hiking and long-distance walks on our travels (when our knees and hips are up to it). On our RTW trip, we did not take hiking boots. Did I miss them? Yes! We had a couple of hikes where my feet, attired in sports shoes, got thoroughly soaked. But I was still glad I hadn't lugged my heavy footwear with me. However, if you're an avid hiker, you might want to bring boots, just as if you are an avid photographer, you will probably sacrifice some clothing or other items for your equipment. Do what makes sense for you.

Whatever you decide to take, don't forget to wear your money-belt to protect your passport, tickets, spare credit card, and cash. If you find a money belt uncomfortable, you can buy T-shirts, bras, shirts, and other clothing with special pockets, as well socks that can hide your valuables.

Should camera buffs go buff?

Kevin is a talented photographer. So when we were planning an African safari years ago, he was in a quandary about which camera equipment to take. We were flying on small planes that would allow only 26 pounds of luggage per passenger. Kevin's lenses and accessories weighed 19 pounds. That left him only 7 pounds for everything else. He went to the camera store to ask if there were some photography items he might reasonably leave behind. "Take everything," the camera-store owner advised. "You might need it. Tell your wife to pack your toothbrush." We have some fabulous photos from that trip, both long shots and close-ups. I leave it to you to figure out whether Kevin took the advice.

Copy your documents.

We always photocopy our passports, in case they are lost or stolen, and keep copies of the list in a compartment in our luggage. (Put them into a PDF form to keep them together.) I also carry a list of our credit card numbers and expiration dates, but I disguise the numbers in an (admittedly) goofy code. For example, let's pretend my credit card number is 4540 0003 7621. My code would be as follows:

Age I was when my nephew married (45)

Plus 40

Plus famous agent minus 4 (James Bond, 007-4 =003)

Centennial (76)

Current age of eldest grandson (21)

Anyone who steals my list will not know my age when my nephew married or what the current age of my grandson is. I disguise my passwords similarly. But be careful — I once forgot my own reference and spent ages figuring it out! You can probably devise a better code. You can also put the information in an accessible cloud-storage space, such as *Dropbox* (**www.dropbox.com**), where, with your password, you can get access to it from anywhere.

Kevin and I take emergency contact information too, along with copies of our prescriptions. Almost everything else (for example, e-tickets) we store in Dropbox, and we leave a copy of our documents with our son.

What other items should you pack?

Here is a list of not-so-obvious items you may want to bring with you:

- A couple of large plastic sacks for laundry or other needs.

- A flat sink stopper and an elastic travel clothesline for lingerie and other washables.

- Dryer sheets — they keep clothing smelling sweet in the suitcase, and they can also be used wet in the sink as laundry soap/conditioner.

- Travel-sized soaps and hand cream.

- Plastic bottle — to be filled with water after passing airport security, saving on buying water at the airport and almost everywhere else.

- Universal plug adapters.

- Safety pins, pinned inside my suitcase. (I'd like to say I also pack a small sewing kit, but I usually forget.)

Everything, no matter how small, adds weight. So I dispose of all packaging and don't use anything but light plastic bags or containers for toiletries. The cute cosmetic bags have to wait for domestic car trips where weight is not an issue.

Yes, you can keep it light!

Remember, when it comes right down to it, all you ever really need to pack are your critical medications, your passport, airline e-ticket numbers, and credit cards. If you're missing something truly essential, you can buy it. So, as the familiar advice goes, when in doubt, leave it out.

Do you have everything? Check again before departure.

Here's a check list to review before taking off:

- ☐ Double-check that your arrangements are complete, and you have left your itinerary, copies of your passport, and other important documents with a designated person.

- ☐ If you want to follow our method for jet-lag, stop drinking coffee and alcohol a few days before your flight. (You can resume drinking coffee again on the plane when it's morning at your first destination. For more on jet lag, see chapter 5.)

- ☐ Be sure you call your credit card companies and tell them where you will be going, so they don't freeze your card and leave you stranded. (If you don't call before you leave and the issuing bank notices charges from a foreign country, your card will be suspended until you contact them.) Also, if you are going on a multi-month trip, some card issuers may require you to call back every few months with an itinerary update.

- ☐ If you need to order a special meal, call your airline at least 24 hours in advance.

☐ Finish packing the night before you leave, so you'll have less to worry about on the day of departure.

☐ Try and get plenty of sleep the night before you leave.

☐ Check to see if your flight is delayed before you leave for the airport. However, sometimes flights can be changed and then be rescheduled to the original time, and if you miss your flight for that reason, the airline is not obliged to compensate you — so keep on top of the latest information.

☐ Before you leave for the airport, make sure you have the airline's customer service number on your phone. If your flight is delayed because of something like mechanical failure, stand in line to talk to the gate agents, but call the airline directly too. You may get through — and be rebooked on another flight — faster by phone. At least you have two avenues for action. (But do review the airline's policy ahead of time. Some airlines allow you to re-book without additional charge if your flight is delayed or canceled, but not all do.) In addition, communicate clearly and politely with the airline's representatives and make sure you're still booked for the return flight, because if you don't take the original outbound flight, the airline will often cancel your return.

☐ Take off with a smile on your face. You're about to embark on one of your life's greatest adventures!

CHAPTER 5:

STAYING HEALTHY
WHILE TRAVELING

Eat healthy foods. (But be careful of salads in less-developed countries.)

Please note that nothing in this chapter is meant as medical
advice. Always consult your own healthcare provider on how to
manage your health while traveling. The information below applies
primarily to those who are healthy or have only minor-to-moderate

health problems. For more serious challenges, you'll find additional resources in the Appendix.

The basic rules of staying well while traveling are to avoid drinking too much alcohol, use sunscreen, wash your hands often or use hand sanitizer, and get plenty of rest. It's easy to overindulge when you're in vacation mode, so moderation makes an enormous difference to your enjoyment of your trip.

Address your medical needs before you go.

As previously mentioned, be sure to visit your doctor at least a couple of months before your planned departure, and share your travel plans. That's especially important if you have an ongoing issue, such as diabetes, heart disease, or kidney problems. If you need to make any changes in your medications, you'll have time to make adjustments before you go.

Ask your physician if he or she can do anything to help your medications last the full length of your trip or at least give you more time before you need to re-order them. Most Medicare drug plans will allow you to get a vacation override to get extra prescriptions, but sometimes they will only provide you with an extra month or two. If that's not sufficient, your doctor may be able to rewrite your prescription in a way that is perfectly legitimate and also fits your needs. For example, my husband's doctor wrote him a prescription "for one or two tablets daily" for a popular medication that allowed him to cut his pills in half and double the length of time before he had to renew them.

You will also want to get copies of your latest prescriptions with the generic names for your medications, in case you lose them and need to refill them abroad. At a minimum, be sure to save your prescription information, along with your doctor's name, phone number, and email address. Keep your prescriptions in their original packages when traveling to avoid problems with TSA or customs.

At your doctor's visit, you can find out how to adjust the timing of your medications as you travel across time zones, which can be critical for the management of certain conditions.

Some people benefit from compression socks to avoid deep-vein thrombosis (DVT), or blood clots in the legs, that may arise when you sit for long periods of time, such as on a plane. But don't assume that's the case! Get your doctor's advice and have the stockings properly fitted, or they may do more harm than good.

In any case, to avoid blood clots when you are sitting cramped up for hours in a plane, get up and move every half hour to an hour when you're awake. Drink extra water (flying is dehydrating), avoid alcohol, wear loose clothes, and practice in-seat exercises. Many airline websites have information on exercises that you can do while seated on the plane. Remember that sitting for long periods in a car or at a desk can cause blood clots too, so taking breaks and moving are good preventative measures anywhere. If you experience persistent leg pain after flying, get checked by a doctor right away.

Another point: if there is any chance you'll be sexually active with a new partner when traveling abroad, remember that sexually-transmitted diseases are no respecter of age or geography. Be prepared. In many countries outside of the western world, condoms may not be of the same quality as at home (or so I've read), so if you need them, buy them domestically.

Visit a travel clinic a few months before you leave.

In addition to visiting your personal physician, it's a good idea to seek out a travel clinic, especially if you plan to travel outside of the more developed areas of the world. The clinic can not only give you the injections you require for your destinations, but they most likely will also be able to provide medications for traveler's diarrhea and antibiotics. That's peace of mind — and money well spent.

What if you need to refill your prescriptions?

If you lose your medications or run short, you'll need to get refills abroad, which isn't always easy. Having a copy of your prescription should help, but be prepared to visit a local doctor and pay for an office call to get a new one. Fortunately, office calls in most countries are cheaper than in the United States. However, be aware that you may have to settle for a drug that is similar to, but not the same, as the one you usually take. Ask your doctor to write your prescription to cover generics, so that won't be an issue.

How many pills do you need?

In some places, filling a prescription for a non-controlled substance is fairly easy. While traveling in Italy, my husband found he had miscalculated and had run out of one of his medications. He requested a copy of his prescription by email from his doctor, but the pharmacist never even asked for it. She simply said, "This is Italy!" and asked him whether he wanted a 30-day or 60-day supply. I have heard that France and Portugal are also fairly lenient on refills, but it's never wise to assume that will be the case.

Refilling a prescription — what's the law?

Legal restrictions vary from country to country, so medications that are legal at home — even over-the-counter medications like ibuprofen or naproxyn (Aleve) — may be illegal in your host country. You'll need to check the laws in both your own country and the nations you plan to visit to see whether your medication can be legally sent from home. For that reason, I can't recommend having a friend or relative mail your prescription.

I have known people who have sent medications (not opioids or other narcotics) overseas without problems. They had a relative mail the pills along with a few cosmetics and odds-and-ends with a note saying, "I'm mailing you the items you left here." It may work, but I'm not recommending that approach.

By the way, common over-the-counter medications can have different names in other countries too, so knowing the generic name will help you. For example, in the United States, acetaminophen is sold under the Tylenol brand; in other countries, it is sold as paracetamol (Panadol).

Increase your exercise.

The one thing you need to do before leaving on a long trip is to increase your exercise. Most likely you will be walking, or standing on your feet, more than usual. So unless your mobility is particularly restricted, try to boost your activity, especially walking, for several weeks before you go, gradually increasing the amount that you do each day.

Try these tips to fight jet lag.

There are many "cures" for jet lag, which most people find worse when flying west-to-east. This is what works for us:

- Cut back on caffeine and alcohol several days before you leave, so that you are completely caffeine-and-alcohol-free for three days before flying.

- Have coffee when it's breakfast time at your destination (often on the plane).

- If you take a nap, keep it short. (We typically shower and nap for no more than an hour or an hour-and-a-half. Obviously, if you arrive at night, you can just go to sleep.)

- Get outside! Exposure to daylight will help you adjust your schedule faster than anything else.

- Stay awake as long as possible, at least until 8 p.m., if you can manage it.

- If your doctor approves, bring melatonin with you if you need help sleeping, but try it before you go to make sure it will work for you. Avoid over-the-counter sleep aids with antihistamines, unless approved by your physician. (A recent study found a link between antihistamine use and dementia. Check WebMD at **www.webmd.com** and search for "Common Meds and Dementia: How Strong is the Link?")

- Take it easy the first day or two. Rome wasn't built in a day, and you shouldn't try to see it in one day, either!

Take a few easy steps to maintain your health while abroad.

Staying healthy while you are traveling is mostly common sense. In most of the western world, or in places like Japan or Singapore, it's doubtful you'll need to worry about the water or food. Otherwise, follow these tips:

- Wash your hands often and/or use hand sanitizer.

- In places where the water is unsafe to drink, drink bottled water. If traveling to remote locales, you may want to bring a small water filter. You can find some lightweight ones at REI and other camping supply stores. (I also drape a small towel over the sink faucet in places where the water is questionable, just as a visual reminder, so I don't absent-mindedly fill a glass of water and drink from it.) Wherever you go, make sure you stay well hydrated.

- If you aren't sure if the food is safe at your destination, eat no fruit or veggies that you can't peel or wash thoroughly in clean water (bottled or boiled). According to the Environmental Protection Agency, water must come to a roiling boil for one minute to be purified. At elevations above a mile (or 2,000 meters), you need to boil water for three minutes to ensure it is safe to drink.

- Cook healthy foods when you are eating in, and cook them thoroughly. (Check out the Centers for Disease Control and Prevention website (*www.cdc.gov*) on "Food and Water Safety" for more information.)

- If you eat street food, choose food that is hot, and look for places that have a high customer turnover, so you know the food has not been sitting out for a long time.

- In questionable areas, go to restaurants and cafes that are recommended in guidebooks. (Even at home, no place is foolproof, but washing your hands often and getting a hepatitis A vaccination can help prevent some food-borne illnesses.)

- You may be advised by friends to take Pepto-Bismol tablets to help prevent traveler's diarrhea. However, according to the Mayo Clinic website, that over-the-counter medication should not be taken for more than three weeks. Don't take it at all if you are allergic to aspirin or without asking your doctor or pharmacist if it will affect your other medications. (For example, don't take it with anticoagulants.) Your doctor or a travel medicine clinic can prescribe prophylactic intestinal medications.

- Maintain your fitness, although you probably won't have to do a lot of formal exercise, because you'll be actively exploring. Still, a few stretches for flexibility or a set or two of push-ups to firm up your arms may help.

- Get plenty of sleep and rest. Take a day off from sightseeing once in a while. Instead of cramming in every museum and attraction, do one major thing, and then take a break. You have the time, so relax.

Learn how to find an English-speaking doctor.

If you have a medical problem that is potentially serious if uncontrolled and you don't speak the language of the country you are visiting, be sure to research both the hospitals near your lodging and identify English-speaking doctors in each city. US embassies in various countries maintain lists of doctors who speak English, and that information is often available online.

Another source is the International Association for Medical Assistance to Travelers (IAMAT) at *www.iamat.org*. You will find health information on its website and, it maintains a directory of English-speaking physicians around the world for its members. There is no fee to join, but IAMAT does ask for a donation.

In an emergency, go to the nearest hospital emergency room (accident and emergency, or A&E, in the UK). In some locations, you may also find walk-in clinics. For example, Florence, Italy, has a walk-in medical facility at 4 Via Roma. The clinic, Health Services Firenze, serves locals and tourists and accepts most travel medical insurance. All the staff speak English.

For a minor health emergency, seek out a large international hotel. The desk staff or concierge should be able to direct you to an English-speaking physician. Many doctors abroad have trained in the US, Canada, or the UK, so it is usually not too difficult to find one who knows English (and probably speaks it better than many native-language speakers).

Do you have a chronic medical condition? It may pay to write down the translations for various medical symptoms or learn the medical terms before you go. It's always good to prepare by knowing the phrases for "I need a doctor/hospital" in the languages of your host countries.

Accept the fact that you may get sick anyway.

Whenever I go on a trip of more than a month, I realize there is a chance I will get some minor illness. Colds, flu, and minor digestive upsets just seem to come with the territory when you're jammed into an airliner or jostled in crowds. For people with compromised immune systems it becomes especially important to eat right and get plenty of sleep.

Packing a few over-the-counter medications for common ailments can help. Having visited a travel clinic before I leave, I typically have antibiotics and antidiarrheal medication with me should I need them. Usually, after a few days of rest, I am ready to go again. The good thing about traveling long-term is that you won't miss out on your entire vacation if you take some time to heal.

The best travel insurance covers medical emergencies abroad, and for non-emergency treatment, medical costs outside of the United States are much lower than at home. You may even be able to find a doctor who will come to your apartment or hotel. If you are a US citizen over the age of 65, your Medicare plan may cover reimbursement for emergency expenses for the first 60 days you are outside of the country. But plans vary, so be sure to check your own coverage. (For more information on travel insurance, see chapter 4.)

Take two aspirin?

If you travel long or often enough, sooner or later, you will become ill in a foreign country. Kevin and I have had some interesting medical experiences abroad over the years, but we have always found professionals who have provided excellent care. Here are a few examples:

- In England in 2015, I awoke one morning with a noticeable droop in my face. I consulted a general practitioner and was sent immediately to a nearby hospital to rule out a stroke. After multiple tests and exams, including a CAT scan and an MRI, I was diagnosed with Bell's Palsy, a common cause of facial paralysis that usually resolves over time. I was prescribed steroids, and I fully recovered. What surprised me the most was that my care, handled as a hospital outpatient, cost me nothing! (There's no guarantee that the UK policy won't change, but at the time, care was free for anyone, even foreigners, as long as the person was treated as an outpatient.)

- While vacationing in Tuscany several years ago, Kevin and I both came down with miserable colds that left our ears stuffed. Fortunately, in Florence, they have a clinic just for foreigners. Kevin went in ahead of me. I walked in a few minutes later to find him stripped to the waist with a beautiful woman doctor examining him. For a long time, he teased me about walking in on him when he was half-naked with another woman! (The doctor gave us decongestants that eased our return plane trip.)

- Once in New Zealand, I came down with a minor infection. Even without insurance, the cost of an office call plus a prescription was less than what my co-pays *with* insurance would have been at home. (Though I'm not sure that's the case today.)

The moral? It's never fun to be sick, but getting sick doesn't have to be a disaster or ruin your vacation.

You can get around in spite of mobility problems.

Although access to public transportation abroad can be more difficult for those with mobility problems, local transportation sites often offer helpful information. (A web search such as "wheelchair accessibility + the city name" or "mobility access + the city name" will usually yield useful sites.)

For example, London Transport offers a map that shows step-free Underground (Tube) stops. In addition, London Transport bus routes all have some kneeling buses with dedicated places for wheelchairs. (See *https://tfl.gov.uk/transport-accessibility/wheelchair-access-and-avoiding-stairs*.)

Unfortunately, in some places the best transportation options for someone with physical challenges often cost much more than public transportation, which can cut deeply into your budget. But if you want to travel independently, just plan more time in less expensive areas and less in cities that are costlier. Isn't it better to reduce the time you spend in a given place than not going at all?

Location makes a difference too. In some areas, such as Southeast Asia, it is not much more expensive to arrange for a car and driver than arranging for a car alone. What's more, *Lyft* (*www.lyft.com*) and *Uber* (*www.uber.com*), companies that enable people with private cars to provide taxi services, encourage their drivers to support those with mobility challenges. Drivers are expected to follow local laws, including those for accessibility. Uber customers can request drivers with vehicles that accommodate both wheelchairs and service animals, and Lyft has a wheelchair policy that says drivers who do not accommodate lightweight wheelchairs may be removed from their system.

Manage other ongoing health problems.

If you have chronic medical issues, you have probably already adopted many routines that will help you travel successfully. Here are some other ideas to deal with specific problems.

Advance planning helps when traveling with a hearing impairment.

Most seniors have some hearing loss, particularly at high frequencies. (They told me that loud rock music would damage my hearing — and they were right!) For those with hearing impairments, traveling can present some frustrations. For one thing, you need to be able to hear boarding announcements for planes and trains, as well as managing your day-to-day reservations and activities. Fortunately, many tours now equip travelers with individual hearing devices or recordings that can be adjusted, which are a big help to understanding.

If you wear a hearing aid, be sure to pack extra batteries and accessories, because it may be difficult to find the right ones in some locations. Pack them in both your carry-on and your checked luggage, too, just in case. And if you expect to travel to a humid climate, consider taking along a dehumidifier for drying your hearing aids at night. For additional travel tips for the hearing impaired, check the website for the American Academy of Otolaryngology (***www.entnet. org/content/travel-tips-hearing-impaired***).

Have a visual impairment? Check out these tips.

If you have a vision problem, among the many good tips offered by MIUSA is to connect with a local organization for the visually impaired where you are traveling. Of course, you'll also want to research public transportation. Be prepared for different attitudes on disability in some countries. While no one wants to be discriminated against or patronized, it's better to know in advance what you might encounter, so you can handle it if it arises. (No, it's not fair, which is why everyone needs to speak up for improved access.) Traveling with a guide dog can also present difficulties, since even service animals can be subject to quarantine in some places, and you don't want to find that out when you arrive. The MIUSA site has advice for dealing with these obstacles at (***www.miusa.org/resource/tipsheet/blindtips***).

The MIUSA site also provides a broad range of information for traveling with many other physical challenges. (See the Appendix.)

Plan ahead to manage your diabetes.

The American Diabetes Association (***www.diabetes.org***) recommends that you see your doctor for a medical exam before you go. The website also advises that you bring a letter from your doctor that explains your condition and lists the medications and devices (such as syringes) that you need, as well as your prescription. If you have any allergies, those should be stated. It's also a good idea to wear a bracelet or other medical ID that identifies you as someone with diabetes. And wherever you go, learn how to say, "I have diabetes" and "sugar or orange juice please," in the local language.

If you use insulin, give some thought to how you will store it on your trip. Although insulin does not have to be refrigerated, it can lose strength in very hot or very cold temperatures. If temperatures are high where you are going, be sure your hotel or apartment has a refrigerator before you book. Alternatively, some hotels will refrigerate your insulin for you — just make sure you can get it when you need it.

Check out more tips on traveling with diabetes by visiting **www. diabetes.org** and searching on the site for "when you travel." You will also find information on "air travel and diabetes" and what you'll need to know about TSA procedures. Always allow extra time for security checks to minimize stress.

Find out where to get an INR test while traveling.

As with all medical conditions, asking your own doctor is the place to start. If you are a cardiac patient who is on Coumadin (warfarin), first make sure you are stable enough to travel. Then, if you need to get a PT-INR test — or any other medical test — while abroad, you can join the International Association for Medical Assistance to Travellers (IAMAT at **www.iamat.org**), which helps members find doctors or contacts for lab work while traveling.

Pack your CPAP machine and supplies.

Do you have sleep apnea? Travelers who need continuous positive airway pressure (CPAP) machines to regulate breathing will need to check their power supply. Many devices support a range of voltages, and if yours does, all you'll need abroad is a plug adapter. (Buy a universal adapter, which contains plugs that work worldwide.) If you have an older machine that works only on 110 volts, you'll also need a voltage adapter. (The voltage will be marked somewhere on the power brick or on the machine itself.) Bring an extension cord, in case there is no outlet near your bed. If your CPAP machine runs on 12 volts, you may also want to take a separate CPAP battery with you. You can find those batteries online.

I've been told that it's usually not difficult to take a CPAP machine, mask, and supplies as hand luggage when you fly. Check with your airline(s); many will let you take your machine as a second carry-on without charge. As with those who carry medications or diabetic supplies, be sure to allow extra time for airport security clearances.

Research where to find incontinence supplies abroad.

According to the CDC, more than 44 percent of people over the age of 65, male and female, suffer from bladder incontinence, which can range from minor stress incontinence (small leakages that occur when you sneeze or cough) to more troublesome conditions.

If you are dealing with incontinence, bring extra supplies and find out where you can get pads, underwear, and other necessary items when you're away. (See resources below.) You may also want to ask your doctor about medications to help ease the feeling of urinary urgency at your pre-travel checkup.

Check to see if the website for your preferred products shows where to buy your supplies abroad. Tena, for example, displays the names of stores that stock its products in several countries. You can also do a web search with the "name-of-the-country + name-of-the-product" to find retail outlets. (For example, entering "Depend + France" displays the company's French site, and with a little help from Google Translate, you can find the stores selling Depend products.)

You may want to look at the Confitex products (***www.confitex underwear.com***) as well and try them out before you leave. This New Zealand company makes washable, highly absorbent underwear and advertises worldwide delivery of its products for men and women. Requiring no pads, these briefs look like normal underwear or attractive lingerie.

Need help finding ostomy supplies?

The United Ostomy Associations of America provides several tips for those who are traveling and need supplies for colostomy, ileostomy, and urostomy at **www.ostomy.org/Ostomy_Travel_Tips. html.** The site recommends a book titled *Yes We Can! Advice on Traveling with an Ostomy and Tips for Everyday Living.* The book, now out of print, may still be available through Amazon.com, Alibris.com, or used-book outlets.

Get assistance for traveling while on dialysis.

The National Kidney Foundation provides several tips on traveling while on kidney dialysis on its website at **www.kidney.org/atoz/ content/traveltip**. Your dialysis center should also be able to help you find locations for receiving dialysis treatments abroad. The Northwest Kidney Centers in Seattle use this website for its patients: **www. globaldialysis.com**, which lists 16,800 dialysis centers in 161 countries.

Prepare for flight delays.

If you have a medical condition that frequently leaves you fatigued, be prepared for occasions when your flight is delayed by bringing a list phone numbers for hotels near your departure airports, especially ones with a free airport shuttle. Then, if your flight is delayed for several hours, you may be able to escape the airport and rest before resuming your journey. Of course, that is much easier to do if you are taking flights within a country where the boarding process does not involve making a repeat visit to immigration control. It will also add to your costs, but sometimes it is worth paying a little more to avoid further problems.

As mentioned above, you may also want to take advantage of the air travel tips on the MIUSA website (***www.miusa.org/resource/ tipsheet/airtraveltips***). Click on the link to the TSA site for advice on air travel at the bottom of the page.

Discover how to travel with more challenging health issues.

While this book focuses mostly on seniors who can navigate with only limited problems, I don't want to leave those with serious physical challenges adrift. If your mobility is severely limited, see the Appendix for more resources.

There is no question that it is more difficult to travel with serious health issues. Even daily life at home requires more planning if you have physical limitations. But barring a severe disability, most people are able to adapt and function, and while I don't want to minimize the issues or the extra preparation involved, committed people with mind-and-body challenges can still savor the joys of travel.

CHAPTER 6:

SIGHTSEEING, SHOPPING, AND EATING OUT

Avoid lines and save time by researching visits to popular sites like The Louvre.

Y ou can get good information on sightseeing, shopping, and eating out in traditional guidebooks, so I will simply add a few tips.

Get a good guidebook for sightseeing.

Although most guidebooks provide useful information on the key sights in major cities or popular areas, I like the *Eyewitness Guides* for planning, because they have extensive photos. However, I wouldn't take those heavy books with me. For European travel, you can't do better than the Rick Steves guides, and his *Europe Through the Back Door* is the premier travel skills book.

I use *Lonely Planet*, as well, because its low-budget approach, aimed at young backpackers, includes useful advice for people of all ages. The same is true of the *Rough Guides and Frommer's*. For historical information, the *Michelin Green Guides* deliver detailed material that you won't find in other travel books. Pick out one or two that you like and expand from there. A good guidebook can tell you what to see, along with why a particular attraction is important, how best to approach it, where to get tickets, and the best times to go to avoid the crowds. Research can help you avoid long queues and save countless hours.

Take advantage of walking tours and local offerings.

Kevin and I often participate in walking tours when we explore a new city. Many of these tours are free and ask only that you pay what you feel the guide was worth. We typically pay about $15 or $20 for both of us. If the tour is especially enjoyable or insightful or if the turnout is low, we may give more. It's sometimes an internal struggle, because we want the guide to benefit, but if we spend a lot more, our budget is in danger. Among the best free city walking tours are those of the city of Bath, England, which set a very high standard. Tour guides in Bath even refuse tips. These expert guides love their historic city and simply want to share it.

For Europe, you can also download free podcasts for self-guided walking tours of some locations. (It's probably easiest to just do a web search on "Rick Steves Audio Tours.")

Global Greeters (**www.globalgreeternetwork.info**) puts you in touch with locals who give you free walking tours beyond the traditional sites, more like seeing a city with a friend. Beginning in New York City in 1992, today there are more than a hundred greeter organizations throughout the world, and the organization is growing. Although the tours are free, many greeter groups are non-profits that appreciate donations. Others are affiliated with official city tourist organizations. We haven't tried Global Greeters, but it's recognized on many budget travel sites.

At the time of this writing, *Icelandair* is offering free "stopover buddies" during the slower winter season. Off-duty Icelandair employees act as your host for one day. It's a warm Icelandic welcome, so I hope they continue to offer the service in the future.

Hop-on, hop-off bus tours can be of good value, but they are an expensive way of going from place to place, so it's usually much cheaper to go between sights by public transit. Still, buses with recorded commentary can serve as an easy introduction to the city. Costs vary, so choose carefully.

Review the *websites of major attractions* in advance. You can usually get directions and often book online to ensure your place. What's more, you can find out if there are any free tours, which many museums offer. Make sure you get the official website; sometimes unscrupulous operators take advantage with a similar site and will charge you more for bookings.

You can, of course, sign up for commercial tours, and if you have a special interest, that type of tour may be worth it. You can also look for alternatives. Sometimes there are other places that can give you a similar experience at less cost.

Here's a quick tale of quokkas and cash.

When we were in Perth on our RTW trip, we planned to take a tour to Rottenest Island. The island is known for its nearly tame quokkas, unique little mammals that live wild only on that island and a couple of other places. However, when we checked the ferry prices, we discovered it would cost us about $100 to get there and back. We had read that Rottenest is a delightful place to go biking, but with my unreliable knee, I can't bicycle. It's also a good place to swim, but Kevin doesn't swim. We realized that we would be coughing up $100 just to see the quokkas! As much as we wanted to see the funny little furballs, we couldn't justify the price when we had a lot more traveling planned. Instead, we went to the Perth Zoo and saw quokkas, koalas, kangaroos, and other unique Australian animals. Best of all, because it was a slow day, we had what amounted to a private tour. John, a charming volunteer in his eighties, had lived in Perth his entire life and loved to tell us all about the wildlife. Our total cost was around $16!

Make your travel dollars stretch.

If you follow our travel style, you'll be renting apartments most of the time and cooking for yourself, which means shopping at the local markets rather than eating out frequently. If you know where to shop, you can save on food and other items.

Ever shop at a dollar store in the US? Well, they have those in Europe, too, but they are called (naturally) euro stores or pound stores (UK) there. If you're not set on a particular brand, or even if you are, buy your toothpaste, soap, and shampoo there. Those stores often have popular brands, or you may find one you like as well. Just make sure that you are really buying shampoo and not dish-washing soap! Like items are grouped together, and by checking *Google Translate* against your shopping list, you'll probably do fine. Toiletries can be very expensive, so it pays to be a bit flexible.

Different locales will offer specialty items at a discount, too. For example, in Paris, don't overlook the money-saving *Picard* chain, which offers all frozen food. This cuisine is not your grandmother's TV dinners! Picard delivers real value and real taste with everything from appetizers and main dishes to desserts.

In Italy, you can save on fresh vegetables and homemade pasta in the markets, plus you can take advantage of *vino sfuso* shops that store wine in barrels or other containers. You can buy clean bottles and have them filled at the shop and bring them back to refill. Some wine varieties are very good and some are only so-so. But the savings are fantastic — typical prices are about €3. Once, *vino sfuso* wine was of inferior quality, but today, many stores get their wine from popular vintners that produce fine wines and simply need a place to get rid of overstocks.

In any country, ask for recommendations from locals. Make sure to ask where they would eat, as opposed to "Do you know a good restaurant?" because if you ask the latter, they may send you to a popular tourist restaurant, assuming you do not want to eat with neighborhood folks. But tourist restaurants will break your budget fast, and those little family-owned places without a tourist menu are more likely to be the ones you'll remember fondly in the years to come.

Avoid tourist shops when buying gifts.

What about shopping for souvenirs or gifts? It all depends on what you are looking for. Do you long for a special handcrafted item as a souvenir? Want to snag a good deal at a flea market? Or do you want high-value goods at a great price? Guidebooks, websites, and friends who have visited the same location will probably be your best bet for advice.

Although they are not the least expensive places to buy local goods, we like government-sponsored shops for buying handicrafts, because they feature select pieces from the most talented artisans in their stores. Granted, you won't find huge bargains there, but you will usually find high quality offerings at a reasonable price.

If you are looking for simple gifts for friends and family, then a supermarket can be your best friend. For example, I have found wonderful hand creams at supermarkets in France, at a much lower price than in the tourist shops. Local street markets are another good source. But don't forget that shipping can add considerably to your cost.

The worst places to shop are the stores in tourist areas. Also, be aware that if you sign up for local tours, the guide may bring you to shops where he or she gets a cut if you buy something. That is not the place to get a deal! In some parts of the world, you will be surrounded by hawkers at tourist haunts or on beaches, and those goods may or may not be of good value.

You will have to firmly say "No," or "No thank you," in the local language to the vendors you don't want to buy from, and just walk on. But be forewarned — it's easier to say that to adults than it is to beautiful, earnest little kids. I remember tearing up in Cambodia, because I couldn't buy every little trinket offered by the sweet-faced children. I knew they might well be the main support of their families. Travel is good for the soul, but it can also be heart-breaking. You simply do what you can. That may include finding a reputable local charity that you can donate to, which will help many people.

One more thing: when you go shopping, be polite and say "hello" and "thank you" in the local language to the shopkeepers. Americans, in particular, are sometimes considered rude tourists because they may ask, "How much is this?" without even bothering with pleasantries. People everywhere appreciate being acknowledged and courtesy goes a long way.

Can you get a VAT refund?

Most of the time, as a budget traveler, I don't spend enough on goods to claim a refund for a VAT (value-added tax), GST (goods and services tax), or a consumption tax. These taxes can be high — often as much as 15 or 25 percent. If you spend enough at one store, you can qualify for a refund on purchased goods. The process is complex, and it differs in each country, so you have to be prepared to go to extra trouble. Even then, you may not be successful, so don't count on getting your money back. You might not be able to find the right office at the airport, or the line can be prohibitively long. And if you decide to use or wear the goods that you bought before you leave the country, they then become used goods, and your refund will be denied. (When I lost a camera in Italy and bought another, I wanted to use it, so I couldn't get a VAT refund.)

However, if you are doing a lot of shopping and you are persistent, you may have better luck. Search "VAT or GST refunds" for the country/countries you want to visit. Just remember wherever you go, if you are going to claim the refund as you leave the country, get to the airport early.

Do your "due diligence" on duty-free.

Is duty-free a good deal? Most travel sites say, "It depends." Alcohol and tobacco products are often much cheaper, but in most cases, electronics are not. To get a bargain at a duty-free shop, research what the item sells for at other stores in the country or online. For example, high-end cosmetics can be a good deal in the country where they are made, but that's not always true. You'll always want to keep in mind the allowance for goods that you can bring into your home country. (See the US Customs and Border Protection website at *www.cpb.gov* and use the search box for "duty-free exemption." Canadians can visit their government website at *www.dutyfreecanada.com/customs-allowances/.*)

APPENDIX:

RECOMMENDATIONS

F ind out how to become more digitally savvy and discover suggestions for devices, websites, and apps in this appendix. You'll also find resources for those who may have special travel concerns, such as people of color, those with disabilities, solo women adventurers, and LGBTQ travelers.

Master the online world.

It's exciting to live during this time of discovery and innovation, and sometimes when I tell my grandchildren about the "way it used to be," I think they find it hard to believe. My family didn't have a TV until I was ten. We had a party-line telephone. What's more, I spent most of my career working in a field (software and digital marketing) that didn't exist when I graduated from high school.

But if the changes excite me, some seniors still feel a little left out of the digital age. If you are reluctant to take advantage of today's technologies, I hope I can help you see the advantages (and relieve your anxiety), because using today's computers and devices can make travel less expensive and far more accessible.

Q: *Where can I learn how to use computers and the web?*

A: Check your local senior center, library, and community college (adult education) for computer courses. If you buy a new computer or tablet, you can also often find classes through the store where you purchased it. (Best Buy and Apple offer training, for example.) Plus, you can find video tutorials on YouTube (*www.youtube.com*) for all computers or devices, including Windows PCs.

The popular "For Dummies" series of books that are available at any large bookstore are another good resource. What's more, AARP has teamed up with Que Publishing to offer several books on smartphones, tablets, computers, and social media. (Search for "AARP + Que Publishing + Technology.")

For some seniors, the biggest obstacles to learning about the online world is the fear of breaking a computer or messing it up completely. That's because we grew up in a mechanical world. Our grandchildren are not troubled by that worry. They seem to have been born with a chip in their brains! However, because this is no longer a mechanical world, it's unlikely you will break a computer just by trying to use it (though you may need to be wary of spilling coffee on your keyboard or device).

Two tricks can make things tick.

My friends in high tech will probably groan over this simple advice, but I include it because time and again, I've found these tips are often overlooked, even by people who are computer literate. If you get stuck or your computer is not working right, the two things I find most useful are to (1) reboot the computer and start over, and/or (2) search the web, if you have a usable computer, for the answer to your specific question.

Q: *I'm afraid to use my credit card online. It seems like taking a big chance.*

A: If you don't want to use your credit card online, that's fine. I don't want to argue with folks who are uncomfortable with that idea, because there are real security risks, although you can minimize them. Just know that if you decide not to use your credit card to book online, you may miss out on many money-saving opportunities. (However, do not use your debit card online, since many banks do not provide the same level of protection for debit cards that they do for credit cards.) Here are my thoughts:

Nothing is completely safe. (Where did we get the idea that everything in the world should be 100 percent safe?) However, I am amazed at friends who frequently use credit cards in restaurants, but refuse to use them online. And guess what? Restaurants and stores are among the most common places where credit-card numbers are stolen. After all, your card can leave your sight for several minutes at a restaurant, and unscrupulous wait staff can steal your number. A friend of mine had her card information stolen at a major department store, where the clerk had installed a skimming device below the counter. My takeaway: Why have a credit card if you're afraid to use it? Why use it in one situation and not in another?

It's also true that credit cards are stolen in massive numbers when hackers break into retail computer systems. So yes, credit card data and identity theft is rising. But there are steps you can take to keep your information somewhat safer.

133

Here are some steps to help protect yourself:

- Do not give your account number to anyone over the phone unless you have made the call.

- Carry your cards (or at least your backup card) in a money belt or other security pouch to minimize losses if someone steals your wallet or purse.

- Keep your eye on your card during a transaction, and make sure you get it back before you leave.

- Never sign a blank receipt. Draw lines through any blank spaces above the total.

- When traveling, check your bills online or by phone to guard against unauthorized use. At home, open bills promptly and review them.

- Report unauthorized charges to the card issuer at once!

You can also check out the Federal Trade Commission website consumer information (*www.consumer.ftc.gov*) on "Privacy, Identity & Online Security."

Another point that bears repeating: make sure you call your credit card issuers before you leave and let them know where you are going, so you don't find your card frozen.

Q: *What computers or electronic devices do you recommend while traveling?*

A: It depends on your needs. If you are using a computer only to look up websites, purchase tickets, or to use email, then a tablet computer may work very well, although the tiny keypad can lead to frustrating typos. (Even a Wi-Fi-equipped smartphone may work, although I prefer the larger screen of a tablet for my aging eyes.) If, however, you expect to perform work on the computer or write a blog, then a small laptop or netbook may be a much better fit. Kevin and I both take both iPad minis and laptops when we travel.

I especially like the fact that with a small tablet, you can not only use email, send messages, and surf the web, but also take advantage of helpful apps to track expenses and navigation, to download books (including guidebooks) or to watch movies.

If you are bringing a tablet and don't have a library card, get one before you go. I was able to download e-books from my local library even while overseas. (See sidebar below "Your tablet is your library" for making the most of your tablet.)

A phone is essential. It doesn't have to be a smartphone, but it needs to be unlocked. (See chapter 4, "Using phones abroad? Choose the solution that works best for you.") A smartphone gives you access to helpful mobile apps, but data costs are extraordinary high when roaming, so you may simply want to use devices that are equipped with Wi-Fi to go online and research information rather than use your mobile phone connection.

Q: **Which travel websites and apps do you recommend most?**

A: Although I have mentioned many websites and apps in this book, the ones listed below are the ones that I find most helpful. Some of these websites also have downloadable apps for your phone or tablets.

For finding flights

Skyscanner: ***www.skyscanner.com***

Kayak: ***www.kayak.com***

AARP Expedia: **www.expedia-aarp.com**

Plus, the airlines' own websites, which I always check last.

For accommodations

Airbnb: **www.airbnb.com**

Booking.com: **www.booking.com**

AARP Expedia: **www.expedia-aarp.com**

Zuji: **www.zuji.com** (for Asia)

For determining distances/time/ costs with various travel modes

Rome2Rio: **www.rome2rio.com**

For train travel across Europe

Loco2: **https://loco2.com**

Deutsche Bahn (German Rail): **www.bahn.com/en/view/index. shtml**

For downloading to your phone (mostly free)

Download these apps at the iTunes store for Apple and at Google Play for devices with an Android operating system:

- *SurfEasy VPN*: Use bank or other accounts online with greatly increased security and privacy with this free VPN (which is critical when using unsecured public networks).

- *Rome2Rio*: Find out how to move from place to place and estimate time and costs.

- *Airbnb*: Discover apartment, home, and room rentals to fit your budget.

- *Citymapper*: Move easily around major world cities (more are added all the time).

- *Via Michelin*: Plan your road trips efficiently.

- *Tripit*: Keep your reservations all in one place for an at-a-glance view.

- *XE currency calculator*: Quickly figure costs in various currencies.

- *Google Translate*: Translate menus and simple communications (can be used offline with downloadable language packs).

- *DuoLingo.com*: Learn the basics of popular languages with this fun and free app.

- *Trail Wallet*: Track your costs with little effort. The only downside to this app is that editing is not intuitive. There is a small charge for the app.

Q: You recommend searching the web to find deals, but can you share some tips on how to search faster?

A: Sure. Some of these tips you may already know, but if not, maybe these will help:

- Use more than one search engine to find information. If you usually use Google search, then also try Bing (***www.bing.com***) or DuckDuckGo (***www.duckduckgo.com***).

- For quick, simple answers, just type your search term on the web search engine. For example, although an app like XE Currency Converter is an easy way to check rates on a number of different currencies, if you simply want to know immediately how much $152 is in euros, try typing "$152 =

euro" in the search box. Or if you want to know what time it is in Beijing, you don't have to go to World Clock, you can just type in "current time in Beijing."

- Make use of plus and minus signs to streamline your search. Here are some examples:

  - Use the minus sign before items you want to exclude from your search. If you want to find accommodations in Rome that exclude hostels, you could enter "Rome accommodations – hostels" into your web search box.

  - Enter the plus sign (+); it works like "and" to combine desired criteria. For example, enter "Rome hotels + bed and breakfast" to find lodging that includes breakfast.

While those are the tricks I use most often, you can find more by entering "make better web searches" in your browser. Take note of the most current information, because search engines get more sophisticated, and easier to use, all the time.

Also, when searching for airfares or hotels, as mentioned earlier, it's a good idea to delete your browsing history before you return to a site. (You can do this on a Windows-based computer under Network and Internet in the Control Panel; on Apple computers and iPads, look under the Safari browser settings and find "Clear History and Website Data.") That's because some web pages will put a *cookie* (which works as a tracker or identifier) on your browser, and then they may not show you the best price on your repeat visit. Supposedly that practice isn't as common as it once was, but it never hurts to be sure.

Q: What guidebooks do you especially recommend?

A: *Lonely Planet* guides are still useful for anyone who wants to travel on a budget. *Rough Guides, Moon,* and *Frommer's* guides are worth checking as well. For in-depth background on the sites and history of a particular city or region, the *Michelin Green Guides* continue to provide scholarly information. I particularly like the *Eyewitness Guides* for initial planning, because they have photos, so they give you a better idea of what you might like to see, although they are text-light. They are good for planning, but I find them a bit too heavy to pack with me.

For European travel, the Rick Steves guides deliver just about everything you would ever need to know. His website (*www.ricksteves.com*), with its travel guides, forums, and travel tips will be very helpful, and, as noted previously, his Europe Through the Back Door (ETBD) crew will even consult on your itinerary planning for a fee. Don't miss his PBS series on Europe. Your library will probably have videos of earlier episodes.

To find information on traveling independently in Europe and learning the skills to navigate your way around and making daily arrangements, pick up Rick Steves *Europe Through the Back Door.* Learn his tips. Many are useful outside of Europe too.

Your tablet is your library.

If you have a tablet computer (iPad or other), check out e-book services like *Scribd* (*www.scribd.com*) or *Oyster* (*www.oyster.com*) that offer subscription services for around $10/month. If you are traveling to multiple locations, those services make it easy to download the latest guidebooks, which can be a real cost savings. Check out which guides are available before you sign up. (It's a good idea to download them before you leave the United States because copyright laws prohibit downloading certain books in some countries.)

Don't overlook your local library. I was able to download e-books from my local library while traveling, although I used Scribd.com too, because the library did not always have up-to-date travel guides. (By the way, your local library may also offer movies for streaming through Hoopla.)

Q: Which tours do you recommend?

A: Kevin and I have mostly traveled independently, with a few exceptions, such as our safari tour of Africa, which was a bit high priced (we could do it cheaper now). The following are tours that friends have taken and recommend:

*Rick Steves European Tours (**www.ricksteves.com/tours**)* are tailored to give participants personal interaction with locals, and his tour leaders consistently get raves. The focus is on encouraging people-to-people travel as a means to understanding and world peace. In 1982, when Rick Steves was just a guy with a backpack (and not the widely known European travel guru he is today), Kevin and I bought our first Eurail Passes from Rick, who helped plan our itinerary. We have been impressed with him ever since!

*Road Scholar tours (**www.roadscholar.org**,* formerly Elderhostel) have been highly recommended by those who favor in-depth educational tours. Many of their offerings are a bit higher priced than my budget, but they offer good value.

Stride Travel (***www.stridetravel.com***) is not a single tour, but a resource that offers search capabilities for more than nine thousand tours in more than one hundred thirty countries. (I have not used it, but it has been featured in major news publications such as the *New York Times* and *Los Angeles Times*.) You can filter your results with a variety of specifications, including the amount you want to pay, locations, lodging, level of physical activity, and type of tour, including "Over 50." It also includes ratings and reviews. (See also tours for those with disabilities below.)

Q: Do you have any other recommendations based on your experience?

A: Our travels frequently take us to Europe, especially the UK, where we once lived. I can also recommend these rental sites:

- *Sykes Cottages* (***www.sykescottages.co.uk***) provides comfortable cottage rentals in England, Wales, Scotland, Ireland, and Northern Ireland with a generous cancellation policy.

- *Helpful Holidays* (***www.helpfulholidays.com***) rents out delightful cottages of character in Devon and Cornwall, but be aware of their very strict cancellation guidelines.

- *The Guardian Holidays Cottages & Villas* (***www.guardian-cottages.co.uk/cottage-collections/***), associated with *The Guardian* newspaper, offers accommodations in the UK, France, Italy, Ireland, and the Channel Islands at a range of prices. (*The Guardian* travel section often features bargains too. It's one of my favorite travel websites.)

Q: You don't mention anything about medical tourism, which is an important consideration for many seniors. Why not?

A: In this book, I have tried to mention only sites and businesses that either I have had a positive experience with, or that friends have recommended, or that have been cited in press articles by travel experts. I don't know enough about medical tourism to recommend any business or site, and some are not reputable. In addition, most surgeries and treatments that are medically necessary are covered by Medicare or private insurance in the United States, although many travelers go abroad to obtain treatments that are experimental or not-yet FDA approved or to get cosmetic surgeries.

Because traditional Medicare plans do not cover dental procedures, many US citizens get dental work done while on holiday in Mexico. Dental care is cheaper there and can be obtained from fully qualified dentists and orthodontists, but unfortunately, I have no recommendations to share for dental tourism at this time.

Q: Although your book is for seniors with only limited health issues, can you suggest any resources for those who have serious disabilities?

A: Yes. While researching this book, I came across a few helpful sites for those with disabilities. I sought in vain for a book that I could recommend, but the reviews on those I found were mixed. If reviewers who are disabled did not find the book helpful, then I could not recommend it either. However, the online world presents more possibilities. Here are some places to check:

- *The US branch of Mobility International or MIUSA* (**www. miusa.org**), as mentioned previously, provides many free resources on its website. Although some of the advice is aimed at younger travelers, it is helpful for others too.

- *Lonely Planet's Accessible Travel Online Resources PDF* includes information on traveling with a disability in countries around the world. Check it out at

  http://media.lonelyplanet.com/shop/media/accessible-travel-online-resources.pdf.

- *Cory Lee's website* (**www.curbfreewithcorylee.com**) is recommended by travel blogger and author Matt Kepnes.

- *John Sage of Sage Traveling* receives the endorsement of travel guru Rick Steves for European travel. Sage provides guides and complete tours for people with disabilities. Check out **www.sagetraveling.com.**

- *Traveleyes* (**http://traveleyes-international.com**) is the first commercial tour operator to provide independent travel for blind and sight-impaired travelers. (One caveat: I don't know anyone who has used this company.) However, it's a promising idea — pairing sighted travelers with visually impaired tour members. The benefit for sighted travelers is that they receive a significant discount for assisting their sight-challenged partners, and those with visual difficulties benefit because they don't have to bring an assistant with them. What's more, Traveleyes travelers often get special privileges. (For example, one group in China was allowed to touch the terracotta warriors in Xian), something standard tours never get to do.)

- *The Disabled Travelers Guide to the World* (**www.disabledtravelersguide.com**) delivers one of the most inspirational websites on travel. Nate and Nancy Berger recount their adventures on every continent — even Antarctica — with Nancy using a wheelchair to sightsee. Even if you're able-bodied, read it to see how the will to travel and the ability to trust can open up the world.

- Finally, the *US Department of State website* features information you should *know before you go* and links to information for disabled travelers at ***https://travel.state.gov/content/passports/en/go/disabilities.html.***

Q: Can you provide any information for LGBTQ travelers? How can we find places that are LGBTQ-friendly?

A: *Lonely Planet* has a PDF that can be downloaded. Do a web search on "Lonely Planet + most gay-friendly places on the planet" to find destinations especially favored by the LGBTQ community. In addition, a web search on "LGBTQ tours" brings up links to everything from adventure travel to more sedate tours of popular locations.

Q: Do you have any information for people of color who are worried about discrimination when they travel?

A: Sadly, racism still exists, and people's experiences vary, even when they share the same background. On his website, Rick Steves includes a discussion on "Travelers of Color in Europe" with several links. (Do a web search on "Rick Steves + Travelers of Color.")

While you are at it, search for Zahra Barnes article "11 Surprising Things about Traveling Abroad as a Black Woman." Barnes recounts her experiences in Turkey with her boyfriend, traveling as a mixed-race couple. Although some of her experience was discomforting—for example, she was often openly stared at — she said, "Was some of what I dealt with annoying?

Yes, undeniably so. Is it going to prevent me from crisscrossing my way across the globe? Absolutely not."

On the other hand, in her blog "Expat Edna," a Pennsylvania native of Asian ancestry recounts how frustrating it can be to be recognized only for her ethnicity and not for her nationality. In Ireland, people complimented her on her English, not realizing she was American, and in China, locals looked down on her because she didn't speak Chinese! What's more, in China, blending in and, as she puts it, looking "the same as 1.3 *billion* other people" and suddenly becoming invisible was "soul crushing." Nonetheless, Expat Edna obviously enjoys her travels. Find her blog at *http://expatedna.com*.

Probably the best suggestion is to ask your own friends of color what their experiences have been at particular destinations, and read travel forums and blogs. I don't want to discount the very real problem of racism in the world, here in the United States or abroad. But I do note that people who travel with an open heart and an open mind tend to have the best travel experiences. I hope you do too.

Q: Do you have any recommendations for senior women traveling solo?

A: I have never made a trip abroad alone, but I hope to one day, because I think you can learn so much about yourself when traveling solo. I have women friends over the age of 50 who have traveled alone, and I have met several single women on personal journeys during our travels.

Almost universally, solo women travelers have said that although they sometimes wish they had someone to share their experiences with, they find that traveling on their own often provides a better opportunity to meet people than traveling with a partner. People tend to reach out to women alone.

It pays to be a bit cautious when traveling solo. Obviously, you want to use your common sense and avoid putting yourself in places or situations that you would avoid at home. (That dark alley, for instance!) Some women also recommend wearing a wedding ring and, if approached in public, casually mention that you are going to be meeting up with your husband or with a friend, so you aren't advertising that you are traveling alone.

If you get a bit lonely, staying in hostels gives you a better chance of meeting other travelers, though many may be younger. Or pick an Airbnb "private room" with a female host who likes to engage with guests. (Most will indicate if they like to do so, and if they are also rated as Superhosts, that's even better.)

I have never failed to be inspired by the plucky solo women travelers I have met, including Linda, a retired teacher that we met in 2015 in Croatia, who each year embarks on a multi-week hiking trip on one of the world's major walks or pilgrimage ways. She has explored El Camino de Santiago de Compostela in Spain, the Pilgrims' Way, and Wainwright's Coast-to-Coast Walk in England, among others. Linda's strategies include getting to know the staff at the hotels and guesthouses where she stays. The desk clerks and others can offer advice on what to see and do, and because Linda engages with them, they are then more aware of her comings and goings, contributing to her safety. She also keeps a photo blog, sending one photo and a brief one-paragraph account of her day, daily, to friends and family, along with information on her next stopping point. That way she maintains flexibility in her travel plans, but she also knows her friends will send up alarms if she fails to report in. Fortunately, when we met her, she had never run into any trouble.

Matt Kepnes' website (***www.nomadicmatt.com***) includes a section on solo female travel with advice and personal accounts, and Rick Steves features "Extra Tips for Solo Women Travelers" on his site (***www.ricksteves.com***) as well. As noted on Steves' site, you rarely hear of single women travelers encountering violence in Europe, and I think that is generally true of most of the world. In many cultures, older women are more respected than in our own, and that alone can contribute to your safety. So don't let the fear of traveling solo hold you back from your great adventure — go!

Blogs for inspiration and information:

Nomadic Matt's travel site
www.nomadicmatt.com

Matt Kepnes' blog is commercial, with books, classes, and resources you can buy. Matt writes mostly for a younger demographic, although he includes good, solid information that anyone can use, and his wholehearted embrace of travel is contagious!

Adventures in Wonderland/a pilgrimage of the heart
https://alisonanddon.com

This blog features the stories of Alison and Don, a retired Canadian couple who began traveling the world in 2011, as they traverse the world. The writing is evocative and the photographs are absolutely stunning. Theirs is a quest of the spirit. While Alison and Don are currently taking a hiatus from travel, even older posts on their blog are worth reading.

Neverending Footsteps
www.neverendingfootsteps.com

Lauren Juliff is a young nomad, who has also been traveling the world since 2011. Her tenacity in exploring the world is remarkable, given that she once suffered from an eating disorder and has experienced severe anxiety attacks. Her style is lively. (One caveat: Like many young people, Lauren occasionally uses words in her blog that may not fit in what we used to call "polite company." However, if you watch cable TV or go to the movies, you are probably used to that by now. I am willing to overlook that because her courage, openness, and youthful enthusiasm are characteristics I would like to emulate.)

Local blogs:

Do a web search for blogs on your destinations. Local blogs have given me some of the most useful tips on what to do and where to go in a city. (Search for "Expat blogs for [your destination]" or "Top 10 blogs for [your destination]" and follow the web bunny-trail. Even commercial blogs, such as those for rental offices in cities, can be helpful.

My blogs:

I wrote these unedited blogs for family and friends to follow us on our travels; hence there are a few typos. (Sadly, I have lost my password and can't go back and make corrections.) Although they were not intended for a wider audience, feel free to take a look.

View from Montmartre *(http://impermontmartre.blogspot. com)*. Discover what we loved about residing for nearly three months in Paris.

Passages (*http://imperpassages.blogspot.com*). Read about our experiences as we made our way around the world.

ABOUT THE AUTHOR

Rachel S. Imper lives in Seattle, Washington, with her husband Kevin. A graduate of the University of Washington, Rachel made her career as a marketing writer and consultant. She and Kevin traveled extensively, both before and after retirement, and have lived for months at a time in Europe and Asia. This book is based on their personal experiences and research. It is offered in the hope that it may help others fulfill their own travel dreams.